The Life of Christ

A Visual Survey

with Dr. William Shell and Artwork by Dr. Lau Waun Kei

DAVID L. DAWSON

D. R. DAWSON

MATTHEW PATTILLO

The Life Of Christ

A Visual Survey

Great Commission Publishing

Great Commission Publishing was launched in December 2002 as an autonomous evangelical religious publishing division of Great Commission Ministries, Inc. Since 1990, Great Commission Ministries has published a broad spectrum of compelling books with life-changing messages including discipleship, Bible study curriculums, leadership materials, women's and men's ministries, family enrichment, as well as proven evangelical materials. We are committed to life-discipleship resources and products that bring glory to God by equipping believers for the work of the ministry through an intense and Holy Spirit empowered process. In 2003, Equipping The Saints became one of five major ministry divisions beneath the Great Commission Ministry umbrella.

Our mission is to bring people all over the world into a relationship with Jesus Christ and into membership in His family as stated in Matthew 28:18-20, to develop people to a Christ-like maturity through studying the Word of God and equipping them for their ministry in the church according to their spiritual gifts and talents, to assist in directing people in a life mission in the world, in order to magnify God's name.

Serving Him together,

Roger McCasland

Great Commission Publishing

For additional information, product descriptions, distribution opportunities, or ordering information please visit our web site at www.greatcommissionpublishing.com.

ISBN 0-9727791-0-8

ETS Ministries is an international organization devoted to helping churches and mission agencies train their saints to do the work of the ministry.

4400 Moulton Street • Suite D • Greenville, Texas 75401 • Toll-Free Phone (888) 577-7739

Fax (903) 454-8524 • Email: etsusa@aol.com • Website: www.equippingthesaints.org

Editor: Matthew Pattillo; Coeditors: Dr. William Shell; Mary Dawson; Typesetting and Graphics: Heather Dawson with Sheri Seawright; Artwork: Dr. Lau Waun Kei; Cover Art: Original print by artist Barry Moser. Used with permission. Cover Design: Heather Dawson

Great Commission
PUBLISHING

Table of Contents

Introduction

The Life of Christ: A Visual Survey relies on the scholarship of A. T. Robertson and John A. Broadus for the division of Jesus' life into 184 events and their placement in a plausible chronology. It allows the reader to examine the life of Jesus from beginning to end as a continuous sequence of events drawn from all four Gospel accounts. Although in a few cases the Gospels remain difficult to reconcile, Robertson's classic work demonstrates in convincing fashion their general agreement and coherence.

With the commentary as a guide, the reader will see where Jesus went, whom He met, and what was said and done. Since it is unavoidalble that in writing a synopsis certain details be abbreviated or ommited altogether, the passages under consideration are referenced so that readers may review the biblical record for themselves. It is strongly suggested that students and teachers alike read and study the relevant passages in each section.

Where quoted text is juxtaposed from different Gospels or from different parts of the same Gospel account an ellipsis has sometimes been used to conjoin the citations. In each case pains have been taken to represent the words of Christ and and those with whom He spoke verbatim.

When the authors of the Gospels wrote their accounts of Jesus' life, they had in mind key emphases and recorded those events that best suited their themes and purposes. One writer omits events that the other writers include, or the same event may be recorded in two or three different ways. It is not unlike a jigsaw puzzle that the reader must put together to see when and where different events occurred and to understand the relationship of individual pieces to the whole story.

To further facilitate study and discussion, the major events have been visualized in a 15-foot chart. This panoramic representation will help readers keep the major events in order while conveying a sense of their narrative thrust and momentum. Students are encouraged to follow the action as it unfolds on maps detailing the scope of events in each chapter. Key verses from the relevant passages have been included on a set of scored cards in the back of the book to aid students in their memorization, study and reflection upon salient themes in each chapter.

Authors of the Gospels

Matthew

Matthew was one of the original twelve disciples called and trained by Jesus and thus an eyewitness to the events of which he writes. He was a tax collector for the Romans, and his orderly record reflects the mind of an accountant. Matthew groups the Gospel materials thematically. Writing to a Jewish audience, he begins with a genealogy demonstrating that Jesus is the legal descendant of both Abraham and David. Matthew relies heavily on the Old Testament, depicting Jesus as the long-awaited Messianic king envisioned by the prophets. His key phrase is, "that it might be fulfilled which was spoken by the prophet."

Mark

Tradition tells us that Mark the son of Mary wrote this Gospel (Acts 12:25). Mark was not one of the Twelve, but was a cousin of Barnabas, the apostle Paul's companion on his first missionary journey (Acts 13:2). He may have been the young man who fled naked at Jesus' arrest (Mark 14:51-52). Mark had wide knowledge of Jesus' life through the disciple Peter, with whom he ministered (1 Peter 5:13). He begins his Gospel with Jesus' baptism by John the Baptist. He is believed to have written for a Roman audience, and portrays Jesus as a man of supernatural power who demonstrated His divine nature through miracles. Mark has given us a capsule of Jesus' life focused on what Jesus *did* rather than on what He *said*. His fast moving account represents Jesus' work and ministry in vivid snapshots introduced by the key word "straightaway" or "immediately."

Luke

Most scholars accept that Luke (the "beloved physician" of Colossians 4:14) was the author of this book. Luke is thought to have been Greek, and wrote his account for a Gentile audience. He was a companion of the apostle Paul on his various missionary journeys, and would have cared for Paul's physical needs on these journeys. Luke's account is notable for its logical and orderly presentation. He begins his Gospel by representing John the Baptist as the fulfillment of Malachi's prophecy of a forerunner to the Messiah. Jesus is Himself portrayed as the prophesied Messiah of the Jews and the universal Savior of the world. Luke focuses on the humanity of Jesus, a loving and caring teacher who reached out to the poor, weak, and outcast of society. Luke alone among the Gospel writers includes a dedication, where he explains that he has personally examined every detail of Jesus' life so that Theophilus, the book's recipient, can be absolutely certain of the truth about Him.

John

John was one of the original twelve disciples trained by Jesus. He was a fisherman and a brother to the disciple James. John describes himself in his Gospel as "the disciple whom Jesus loved." Where the other Gospels walk the reader through events in the life of Jesus, John's Gospel takes as a starting point Christ with God before the world began and develops a more theological and evangelistic presentation of His life and mission. His expressed purpose is "that you may believe that Jesus is the Christ, the Son of God, and that believing you may have life in His name" (John 20:31). John deals more comprehensively with what Jesus *said* than with what He *did*, and tries to guide the reader to the logical conclusion that Jesus was God incarnate — the God who became flesh and dwelt among us.

Announcements to Zacharias, Mary, and Joseph

This chapter deals with the pre-incarnate existence of Jesus in heaven, the appearance of the forerunner of the Messiah, as well as other prophetic events related to the coming of the Messiah. Also addressed here are the events of Jesus' birth and early life until the beginning of His public ministry.

About 5 B.C.

PRELUDE TO THE BIRTH OF CHRIST

Luke's Dedication to Theophilus

Luke begins his Gospel by explaining to Theophilus, the book's recipient, his intention to set out an orderly account of Jesus' life and ministry. It will be founded upon the testimony of eyewitnesses so that Theophilus will know with certainty the things he has been taught about Jesus.

◀ Luke 1:1-4

The Incarnation

John begins his Gospel with an unambiguous declaration that Jesus is God "in the flesh":

◀ John 1:1-18

> In the beginning was the Word, and the Word was with God, and the Word was God. He was in the beginning with God. All things were made through Him, and without Him nothing was made that was made…And the Word became flesh and dwelt among us, and we beheld His glory, the glory as of the only begotten of the Father, full of grace and truth.
> — John 1:1-3,14

The teaching that Jesus is deity incarnate, among us as one of us, in flesh, blood, time, and space, becomes a central, organizing tenet of the Christian faith. The radical nature of this claim, with its mind-boggling implications for the meaning of life, has both fascinated and scandalized human discourse since the first moment of its inception. Among the many titles John uses for Jesus, the first is "the Word." It is worth briefly recapitulating some essential truths about the Word presented in John's introductory statements:

- The Word was in the beginning
- The Word was with God.
- The Word was God.
- The Word became flesh and dwelt among us.

John states that it is through the Word that all things came into being. As the very Word of God, Jesus is represented as the agent and effective force in the act of creation. The opening words of his Gospel are an unmistakable echo of those with which the creation account in Genesis is commenced (see Genesis 1:1). John tells us further that "in Him was life" itself, shining as light in an uncomprehending darkness. It is this "true Light" which coming into the world "gives light to every man."

Two Genealogies

Matthew 1:1-17 ▶
Luke 3:23-38 ▶

Matthew is writing to a Jewish audience made up of both believers and nonbelievers, and so begins with Jesus' genealogy in order to demonstrate that He was a legal descendant of both Abraham and David. Because of the explicit promises given by God to Abraham that the Messiah would be one of his descendants (see Genesis 12:1-3; 2 Samuel 7:12-16), it was necessary that Jesus stand in the line of the patriarchs to be recognized and accepted as the promised Savior-King of Israel.

Messiah is a Hebrew word meaning *anointed*, or *anointed one*, indicating His kingly and priestly responsibilities. The Greek equivalent of the word is, *Christ*. The central thread of the Hebrew Bible traces the history of the people God used to fulfill His promise of a coming Messiah. The genealogies of Matthew and Luke include many of its major figures. Many scholars attribute the differences in the genealogies of Matthew and Luke to the fact that Matthew traces his genealogy through Joseph to David and Abraham, while Luke begins with Mary and follows the genealogy through David and Abraham to Adam.

Announcement to Zacharias

Luke 1:5-25 ▶

The last book of the Old Testament was scribed by the prophet Malachi. It closes with a promise:

> Behold, I will send you Elijah the prophet before the coming of the great and dreadful day of the Lord. And he will turn the hearts of the fathers to the children and the hearts of the children to their fathers. — Malachi 4:5-6

This prophecy is fulfilled with the annunciation of the Messiah's forerunner John. Zacharias, an elderly priest in Israel, is commissioned one year to burn incense before the altar of God. Luke tells us that with "the whole multitude praying outside" Zacharias enters into the holy place of the Temple where the altar of incense is situated. There he receives the shock of his life when the angel Gabriel appears to him "standing on the right side of the altar" and declares that his prayers and those of his childless wife, Elizabeth, have been heard. She will bear a son whom they are to call John. Gabriel tells him that John is to go before the Lord's face in the spirit and power of Elijah, to turn the hearts of the people to God and to prepare them to receive their Messiah.

Zacharias, protesting, "I am an old man, and my wife is well advanced in years," asks for assurance that these things will happen. "I am Gabriel, who stands in the presence of God, and was sent to speak to you and bring you these glad tidings," the angel replies. "But behold, you will be mute and not able to speak until the day these things take place because you did not believe my words." Zacharias emerges from the Temple speechless but gesturing to the people, who ascertain that he has seen a vision. He will be unable to speak until the foretold events become reality

Announcement to Mary

◀ Luke 1:26-38

Six months later, God sends the same messenger to Mary, the young fiancée of Joseph, a man of the house of David. Gabriel greets the surely startled and awestruck teenager as "highly favored one" and announces to her that she has been chosen to bear God's Son, whom she is to call Jesus. He will be great and will be called the Son of the Most High, and will be given the throne of His father David (see 2 Samuel 7:12-16; Psalm 132:11). He will reign over the house of Jacob forever and His kingdom will have no end.

Mary asks how this can be, since she is a virgin. "The Holy Spirit will come upon you, and the power of the Highest will overshadow you," Gabriel replies. "That Holy One who is to be born will be called the Son of God." Mary is then told about her cousin Elizabeth, who is six months pregnant and is likewise to have a son. Consenting to all God has divulged through the archangel, Mary answers: "Behold, the maidservant of the Lord! Let it be to me according to your word."

Mary's Visit to Elizabeth

◀ Luke 1:39-45

She departs Nazareth with haste to visit Elizabeth and Zacharias in the hill country of Judea, a considerable journey of some 60 to 70 miles. Luke writes that when Mary arrives and greets Elizabeth, the baby in Elizabeth's womb leaps for joy and Elizabeth is filled with the Holy Ghost and prophesies: "Blessed are you among women, and blessed is the fruit of your womb!"

The Magnificat

◀ Luke 1:46-56

Mary responds in words of praise to God now referred to as the *Magnificat*. She remains with Elizabeth about three months, until Elizabeth is ready to deliver her son, then returns to her home in Nazareth.

The Birth of John the Baptist

◀ Luke 1:57-80

The forerunner of the promised Messiah is born and named eight days later. At the circumcision, relatives and neighbors move to have him named Zacharias after his father, but Elizabeth insists that he be called John. When asked, Zacharias confirms by writing on a tablet, "His name is John," in accordance with the archangel Gabriel's command. Instantly, Zacharias' "mouth was opened and his tongue loosed" and, filled with the Holy Spirit, he prophesies. His words are preserved for us by Luke in a prayer called the *Benedictus*. Addressing his newborn son, Zacharias declares: "you child, will be called the prophet of the Highest; for you will go before the face of the Lord to prepare His ways."

Matthew 1:18-25 ▶

Announcement to Joseph

Matthew provides us with the details of how Joseph comes to know about Mary's part in God's plan. His Gospel confirms that the relationship between Mary and Joseph was unconsummated at any time prior to the birth of Jesus. Joseph is then understandably disconcerted by the discovery that his young intended is with child and he is "minded to put her away secretly" rather than go through a public scandal.

He is mulling over this unhappy development and considering a discreet withdrawal of his marital intentions toward her when an angel appears to him in a dream and says, "Joseph, son of David, do not be afraid to take to you Mary your wife, for that which is conceived in her is of the Holy Spirit." Mary will have a son who is to be named Jesus. He will save His people from their sins, as indeed the very name *Yeshua* (Jesus) in Hebrew means, *Yahweh saves*.

The angel further reveals to Joseph that this strange birth will be a fulfillment of Isaiah's prophecy that "the virgin shall conceive and bear a Son and shall call his name Immanuel" (Isaiah 7:14), a word which translated means *God-with-us*. Like Mary, Joseph willingly accepts the angelic declaration and "being aroused from sleep he did as the angel of the Lord commanded," marrying the virgin. He had not had sexual relations with her when she gives birth to a son.

About 4 B.C.

 # FROM HEAVEN TO BETHLEHEM

Luke 2:1-7 ▶

The Birth of Jesus

The birth of Jesus occurs during the reign of the Roman Caesar Augustus. Rome has dominated the region of Jesus' birth since Pompeii took Jerusalem from the Hasmonean kingdom in 63 B.C. Around 4 B.C., Augustus calls for a census of his empire. In compliance with the requirements of the census, Joseph travels from Nazareth in Galilee to Bethlehem, a small town outside Jerusalem, so that he and Mary can be registered in the town of his ancestry. They find the inns are filled and the baby Jesus is born in a stable. This birth in Bethlehem is foretold centuries earlier by the prophet Micah:

> But you, Bethlehem Ephrathah, though you are little among the thousands of Judah, yet out of you shall come forth to Me the One to be Ruler in Israel, whose goings forth are from of old, from everlasting.   —Micah 5:2

Adoration of the Shepherds

◄ Luke 2: 8-20

The announcement of Jesus' birth is not made to the religious leaders of Israel, but a radiant angel is sent instead to shepherds caring for their flocks in the fields. The angel declares to them the birth of "a Savior, who is Christ the Lord." Lying in a manger in the City of David they will find "a Babe wrapped in swaddling clothes." This is He. All of a sudden there appear with the angel a multitude of angels praising God. Then, just as suddenly, they vanish away into heaven.

Jolted by the sight of thronging angels and the blast of the Christmas revelation, the shepherds leave their sheep and hurry into Bethlehem where they find Mary and Joseph with the baby. Here, they disclose all the angels revealed to them and "those who heard it marvelled at those things which were told them by the shepherds."

The Circumcision

◄ Luke 2:21

Jesus is circumcised on the eighth day in fulfillment of God's command to Abraham and his descendants (see Genesis 17:12-13), and is named as instructed by the angel. Like other Jewish parents, Jesus' parents place Him under obligation to the Law, that He might receive all the privileges and blessings it entails.

2   BETHLEHEM TO JERUSALEM AND BACK

Presentation in the Temple

◄ Luke 2:22-38

Mary and Joseph journey north six miles to Jerusalem where Jesus is presented in the Temple on the fortieth day. There, in accordance with the Mosaic Law, Mary is ceremonially cleansed, and Jesus is consecrated to God as the firstborn (see Leviticus 12:1-8; Numbers 18:16). Simeon and Anna, two devout and elderly worshipers, are present that day.

The Holy Spirit has revealed to Simeon that he will not "see death before he has seen the Lord's Christ." Recognizing in the Baby Jesus the fulfillment of this promise he takes the child into his arms, blesses God, and prophesies about Jesus' life and ministry: "Behold this child is destined for the fall and rising of many in Israel." He adds a comment about the suffering Mary will endure: "Yes, a sword will pierce through your own soul." Simeon's prayer to God is known to us as the *Nunc Dimittis* ("I am ready to depart"), and designates Jesus as "Your salvation . . . prepared before the face of all peoples, a light to bring revelation to the Gentiles, and the glory of Your people Israel." Luke describes Anna as an 84-year-old prophetess and widow "who did not depart from the temple, but served God with fastings and prayers night and day." She hears Simeon's prophecy and realizes that the Messiah she has sought is here, and she too gives thanks to God. Mary and Joseph then return to Bethlehem.

Matthew 2:1-12 ▶

Adoration of the Magi

In Matthew's narrative we learn of wise men or magi commonly believed to be visiting the city of Jerusalem from the East beyond the boundaries of the Roman Empire. It is only fitting that a King of the Jews have foreign dignitaries recognize His royal birth and so it is that the Magi arrive from many hundreds of miles away in search of Him "who has been born King of the Jews." Upon their arrival in Jerusalem they begin to inquire where He may be found since they "have seen His star in the East and have come to worship Him."

When King Herod learns of this he is troubled and asks the chief priests and scribes of the people where the Messiah is to be born. They reply that Bethlehem in Judea is the prophesied birthplace. Herod instructs the wise men to find the child and then report to him His location and identity. This, ostensibly, so that he might himself pay homage to the king. The wise men hear King Herod out and depart for Bethlehem with the star which they had seen in the East leading the way. With "exceedingly great joy" they observe the star coming to a standstill above the house where they will find Him.

Matthew writes that "when they had come into the house, they saw the child with Mary His mother, and fell down and worshiped Him." They further "opened their treasures," bestowing opulent gifts as a tribute and recognition of Jesus' kingly prerogatives, but they depart home by another way when divinely warned in a dream not to return to Herod news of the child's whereabouts.

3   BETHLEHEM TO EGYPT

Matthew 2:13-18 ▶

Escape to Egypt

No sooner have they departed than "an angel of the Lord" appears to Joseph in a dream. The angel instructs him to "arise, take the young child and His mother and flee to Egypt, and stay there until I bring you word; for Herod will seek the young child to destroy Him." Joseph departs for Egypt to evade the king's paranoid designs on Jesus' life. It is a surely anxious and furtive escape by night to the border some 110 miles away. Matthew tells us that this relocation to Egypt is foretold by the prophet Hosea who wrote, "out of Egypt I called My son" (Hosea 11:1).

When he realizes the wise men have neatly eluded him, an enraged Herod commands that every male under two years of age be put to death in Bethlehem and the surrounding region. This massacre is itself foretold in the Hebrew Bible prophecy when Jeremiah depicts the inconsolable mothers whose children perish under Herod's murderous decree: "A voice was heard in Ramah, lamentation and bitter weeping. Rachel weeping for her children, refusing to be comforted for her children, because they are no more" (Jeremiah 31:15).

4   EGYPT TO NAZARETH

Return to Galilee

Some time later, after Herod's death, an angel appears to Joseph in a dream and commands him to return to Israel. Herod's son Archelaus has acceded to the throne in Judea, so Joseph, warned yet again in a dream, moves his family to Nazareth in Galilee instead. It is possible that Joseph had not returned to Nazareth since Jesus' birth. Matthew writes that their arrival in this city is in accordance with the prophecy that the Messiah shall be called a Nazarene.

◄ Matthew 2:19-23
◄ Luke 2:39

Jesus' Childhood

The only knowledge we have of Jesus' childhood years in Nazareth is from the Gospel of Luke, where we learn that Jesus "became strong in spirit, filled with wisdom" and that "the grace of God was upon Him."

◄ Luke 2:40

5   NAZARETH TO JERUSALEM AND BACK

Jesus Among the Doctors of the Law

At age 12, Jesus travels to Jerusalem with His parents to attend the annual Passover feast, a journey of some 90 miles. The Torah, given on Mount Sinai to Moses by God, required all Jewish males to attend the feast in the holy city each year. Jesus was now old enough to be considered personally responsible for the keeping of the Torah. After the feast, Mary and Joseph depart Jerusalem "supposing Him to have been in the company" among their relatives and acquaintances. Luke tells us that in fact the boy Jesus lingered behind in Jerusalem. When at the end of a day's journey Mary and Joseph realize that Jesus is not with them, they return to the city.

◄ Luke 2:41-50

On the third day of an anxious and otherwise unavailing search for Jesus, His parents enter the Temple where they find Jesus sitting in the midst of the teachers and conversing with them, both listening to them and asking them questions. Luke writes that "all who heard Him were astonished at His understanding and answers." When confronted by His mother complaining, "Son, why have you done this to us?" Jesus replies, "Why did you seek Me? Did you not know that I must be about My Father's business?"

The Eighteen Years at Nazareth

Jesus returns home to Nazareth with Mary and Joseph. On Jesus' life from age 12 until the beginning of His public ministry some 18 years

◄ Luke 2:51-52

later the Scriptures are silent except for Luke's statement that Jesus "increased in wisdom and stature and in favor with God and men." The Gospel accounts suggest that Joseph may have apprenticed Jesus in his trade as a carpenter (see Matthew 13:55; Mark 6:3).

Conclusion

The supernatual power exhibited in the birth of Jesus and in the events surrounding His early life, together with the numerous corroborations of the prophetic Scripture make clear that this is no ordinary human being.

Map of Palestine at
the time of Christ

Damascus

Sidon

Mt Hermon

Dan • Caesarea Philippi

Tyre

PHOENICIA

The
Mediterranean
Sea

GALILEE

Chorazin

CAPERNAUM   • Bethsaida

Sea
of
Galilee

CANA
Magdala
Tiberias • Gergesa

NAZARETH

Mt Carmel

Mt Tabor

Nain

DECAPOLIS

— ·· — ·· — Extent of the Kingdom
of Herod the Great

SAMARIA

Caesarea

Samaria   Sychar

Shechem

Ephraim

Bethel

PEREA

Joppa

Emmaus   Jericho   BETHABARA

JERUSALEM   Bethphage

Bethany   Qumran

BETHLEHEM

JUDEA

Gaza   Hebron

RIVER JORDAN

The
Dead
Sea

To Egypt

miles
0   10   20   30

0   10   20   30
kilometers

The Beginning of Jesus' Public Ministry

In this chapter we encounter Jesus at age 30 on the brink of His public ministry. We will witness His baptism and testing, the calling of six men, His first miracle, His first teaching at Jerusalem, and a public declaration of His messianic identity.

Spring, A.D. 26

Historical Background

Before we examine Jesus' ministry, we must return to John the Baptist's ministry of preparation. "The word of God came to John" during the reign of the Roman Caesar Tiberius, when "Annas and Caiaphas were high priests" in Israel.

◀ Mark 1:1
◀ Luke 2:1-2

John the Forerunner

Mark begins his Gospel by reminding us of prophecies in Malachi and Isaiah foretelling the coming of a forerunner to the Messiah. From Malachi he notes a divine promise: "Behold, I send my messenger, and he will prepare the way before me" (Malachi 3:1). From the prophet Isaiah he cites a passage that reads, "The voice of one crying in the wilderness: 'prepare the way of the Lord; make straight in the desert a highway for our God'" (Isaiah 40:3). In Mark's Gospel these prophecies are explicitly tied to John's ministry.

◀ Matthew 3:1-6
◀ Mark 1:2-6
◀ Luke 3:3-6

Mark depicts John living in the wilderness, clothed in camel's hair with a leather belt around his waist, surviving on a diet of locusts and wild honey. Led by the Spirit of God, he calls on the people in the region of the Jordan to repent because the Kingdom of God is at hand, and to be baptized as a sign of repentance. People come from Jerusalem and all over Judea to confess their sins and to receive baptism by John.

John's Call to Repentance

From the banks of the Jordan John upbraids the Pharisees and Sadducees thus: "Brood of vipers! Who warned you to flee from the wrath to come?" He goads them to "bear fruits worthy of repentance," and warns against depending on ancestral ties to Abraham for salvation since "God is able to raise up children to Abraham from these stones." John prophesies that judgment is coming and that "even now the axe is laid to the root of the trees." Only trees producing good fruit will be spared while every other is "cut down and thrown into the fire."

◀ Matthew 3:7-10
◀ Luke 3:7-14

Alarmed by John's warning, the crowds ask what they must then do.. John exhorts them to be charitable to those in need: "He who has two tunics, let him give to him who has none; and he who has food let him do likewise." Tax collectors soliciting John for advice are told to stop extorting more than they are owed. "Likewise the soldiers asked him, saying, 'And what shall we do?'" John tells them to stop using their power to falsely accuse and intimidate people. "And be content with your wages." True repentance demonstrated by righteous living is the key to God's kingdom.

John Heralds the Messiah

Matthew 3:11-12 ▶
Mark 1:7-8 ▶
Luke 3:15-18 ▶

John's teaching so electrifies his listeners that they "were in expectation" and "all reasoned in their hearts about John, whether he was the Christ or not." He clarifies his role as that of the Messiah's predecessor, announcing that "One mightier than I is coming" since "I indeed baptized you with water," while "He will baptize you with the Holy Spirit and fire." The external sign of water baptism will be fulfilled by the internal reality of baptism in the Holy Spirit. But there is a note of warning in this as well, since He will "gather His wheat into the barn" but will "burn up the chaff with unquenchable fire."

Fall, A.D. 26

6 NAZARETH TO BETHABARA ON THE JORDAN RIVER

The Baptism

Matthew 3:13-17 ▶
Mark 1:9-11 ▶
Luke 3:21-23 ▶

As Jesus begins His public ministry, He travels south from His home in Nazareth of Galilee about 60 or 70 miles to the Jordan River near Bethabara (or Bethany), where John the Baptist is preaching and baptizing. Overruling John's objections, Jesus presents Himself for baptism. "Coming up from the water," Jesus sees "the heavens parting and the Spirit descending upon Him like a dove." At this moment a voice from heaven utters the words, **"You are My beloved Son; in You I am well pleased."** Mark writes that "immediately the Spirit drove Him into the wilderness" of Judea with the wild beasts where He is tested by Satan. Luke records that Jesus is thirty years of age at this time.

7 BETHABARA TO THE WILDERNESS

The Temptation

Matthew 4:1-11 ▶
Mark 1:12-13 ▶
Luke 4:1-13 ▶

Jesus is led by the Spirit of God west into the Judean wilderness for 40 days and 40 nights and is tempted there by Satan. He fasts for the duration of this period and by the end is both tired and famished. "If You are the Son of God, command that these stones become bread," Satan baits Him. Jesus answers with a citation from the book of Deuteronomy: "Man shall not live by bread alone; but man lives by every word that proceeds from the mouth of the Lord" (Deuteronomy 8:3).

The devil then conveys Him "into the Holy City [and] set Him on the pinnacle of the temple. Foiled once by Jesus' skillful use of Scripture, Satan cunningly insinuates a reference from the Psalms into his next appeal. "If You are the Son of God, throw Yourself down." After all, his argument goes, the Father "shall give His angels charge over you, to keep you in all your ways. In their hands they shall bear you up, lest you dash your foot against a stone" (Psalm 91:11-12). Jesus recognizes this as a presumptuous misuse of the passage and counters with a verse from the Law, deftly exposing Satan's malignant intent: "You shall not tempt the Lord your God" (Deuteronomy 6:16).

Jesus is tempted yet again when Satan takes Him onto an "exceedingly high mountain" and shows Him "all the kingdoms of the world and their glory" in a dazzling panorama, propositioning Him thus: "All this authority I will give You and their glory; for this has been delivered to me and I give it to whomever I wish. Therefore if You worship before me, all will be Yours." "You shall fear the Lord your God and serve *Him*," (Deuteronomy 6:13) Jesus answers.

Thwarted, Satan departs for a season and angels minister to Jesus. Many years later the author of the letter to the Hebrews will observe that "we do not have a High Priest who cannot sympathize with our weaknesses, but was in all points tempted as we are, yet without sin" (Hebrews 4:15).

The Interrogation of John

◄ John 1:19-28

Acutely aware of the Old Testament prophecies and the messianic expectation of the people, the Jewish religious leaders become concerned about John's ministry and his popularity. Priests and Levites from Jerusalem are sent to inquire of John, "Who are You?" "I am not the Christ," John tells them.

"What do you say about yourself?" they press him. Is John the "Elijah" of Malachi's prophecy (see Malachi 3:1; 4:5), or "the Prophet" that God told Moses He would raise up (see Deuteronomy 18:15)? John resists on both guesses, identifying himself instead as the forerunner to the Messiah prophesied by Isaiah: "The voice of one crying in the wilderness, Make straight the way of the Lord" (Isaiah 40:3).

The religious leaders demand to know on what authority John is baptizing. John replies that although he baptizes with water, there is One among them "whose sandal strap I am not worthy to loose." All of this transpires in Bethany beyond the Jordan.

Winter, A.D. 26/27

John 1:29-34 ▶

John 1:35-51 ▶

John 2:1-11 ▶

8 THE WILDERNESS TO THE REGIONS OF BETHANY

John's Messianic Witness

The very next day John sees Jesus, returned from His 40-day fast and temptation in the Judean wilderness, and testifies: "Behold! The Lamb of God who takes away the sin of the world . . . I saw the Spirit descending from heaven like a dove and He remained upon Him." This is the sign by which God promised to reveal the Messiah to John. "I have seen and testified that this is the Son of God," John announces. "This is He who baptizes with the Holy Spirit."

First Disciples

On the following day John sees Jesus and says to two of his disciples, "Behold the Lamb of God!" The two disciples follow Jesus. "Rabbi, where are You staying?" they ask. "Come and see!" Jesus replies. One of the two, Andrew, finds his brother Simon and says to him, "We have found the Messiah." Andrew then takes Simon to Jesus. "You are Simon the son of Jonah," Jesus says to him. "You shall be called Cephas" (or Peter, which means "rock").

While preparing to depart Judea for Galilee Jesus meets Philip, a fellow from Andrew and Peter's hometown, Bethsaida. After receiving Jesus' invitation to follow Him, Philip finds Nathanael under a fig tree and tells him they have found the foretold Messiah: "Him of whom Moses in the law, and also the prophets, wrote—Jesus of Nazareth, the son of Joseph." "Can anything good come out of Nazareth?" Nathanael retorts. "Come and see," Philip says. When Jesus meets Nathanael He says to him, "Behold, an Israelite in whom there is no deceit!" "How do you know me?" Nathanael replies. "Before Philip called you, when you were under the fig tree, I saw you," Jesus says. "Rabbi," Nathanael answers, awestruck by this lesser miracle, "You are the Son of God! You are the King of Israel."

"Because I said to you, 'I saw you under the fig tree,' do you believe?" Jesus wonders. Nathanael will "see much greater things than these," including "heaven open" and "the angels ascending and descending on the Son of Man." Jesus then departs Judea for Galilee.

9 THE REGIONS OF BETHANY TO CANA

The Wedding Feast at Cana

Jesus heads north into Galilee. In Cana He is invited to attend a wedding where His mother is in attendance. Cana is a small town about five miles north of Nazareth. When the supply of wine is exhausted she prevails on Him to help. "They have no wine," Mary says to Jesus. "Woman, what does your concern have to do with Me?" Jesus protests. "My hour has not yet come." Mary turns to the servants. "Whatever He says to you, do it," she tells them.

Jesus, relenting, orders that six pots used for purification rituals be filled with water, a combined volume of about 150 gallons. "Draw some out now, and take it to the master of the feast," Jesus says. The water is miraculously changed into wine of such excellence that the master of the feast is amazed. Calling the bridegroom he chides him for reserving the "good wine until now" when it is commonly the inferior vintage that is served last, after the guests are "well drunk." By this festive sign Jesus announces the coming of the Kingdom as God's Son, compelling the disciples present to recognize His messianic identity and mission.

 CANA TO CAPERNAUM

Journey to Capernaum

◀ John 2:12

Jesus next departs Cana and heads northward for Capernaum with His mother and brothers, a journey of about 20 miles. His new disciples, several of whom live in Capernaum, accompany them. They remain in Capernaum for a time, and this city becomes a center for Jesus and His disciples during His earthly ministry.

 CAPERNAUM TO JERUSALEM

Spring, A.D. 27

Cleansing of the Temple

◀ John 2:13-22

Soon after their arrival in Capernaum Jesus travels south to celebrate Passover with His disciples in Jerusalem. In the Temple He finds money changers and those selling "oxen and sheep and doves" for sacrifice. With "a whip of cords" Jesus violently expels them from its premises, driving "them all out of the temple, with the sheep and oxen," upsetting their tables and pouring out the changers' money. He orders the dove sellers to "take these things away" and rails at the lot for making "My Father's house a house of merchandise!" A passage from a psalm of King David suggests itself: "Then [His disciples] remembered that it was written, 'Zeal for Your house has eaten me up'" (see Psalms 69:9).

The doubtless alarmed and irate Temple leaders demand proof of Jesus' authority to purge the Temple and rout its traders: "What sign do You show us, since You do these things?" "Destroy this temple and in three days I will raise it up," Jesus retorts. But "it has taken 46 years to build this temple," they jeer, "and will You raise it up in three days?"

Misjudging the intent of Jesus' challenge, the Jews are merely appalled by what seems to them a claim at once reckless and irreverent. Much later, when Jesus is raised from the dead, His disciples remember His words and realize that He indicated by them not the religious edifice in Jerusalem but the temple of His own body. The fulfillment of Jesus' prophetic challenge in the events of His death and resurrection will further substantiate and confirm their faith.

Jesus and Nicodemus

John 2:23–3:21 ▸

John records that many at the Passover festival come to believe because of the signs Jesus performs. Because the priests had responsibility to examine signs and guide the people as to their validity, a person could not simply do as he wished in the Temple without their permission. Jesus' cleansing of the Temple would have created a great stir among the religious leaders and people alike. It must have had a profound impact on individuals such as Nicodemus, whom we meet in John's Gospel coming to Jesus by night to decide the question of just who He is.

Nicodemus is himself a Pharisee and may well have been a member of the Sanhedrin, the council of 70 men guiding the spiritual affairs of Israel. Nicodemus greets Jesus as "Rabbi" and acknowledges that "no one can do these signs that You do unless God is with him." Discerning the real questions on Nicodemus' heart, Jesus abruptly announces that "unless a man is born again he cannot see the kingdom of God."

"How can a man be born when he is old?" Nicodemus asks. "Can he enter a second time into his mother's womb and be born?" Jesus answers that a man must be born of his mother, "of water," first, and then have a second, spiritual rebirth. "Most assuredly I say to you, unless one is born of water and the Spirit, he cannot enter the kingdom of God," Jesus says. "What is born of flesh is flesh, and what is born of Spirit is spirit." Those born of the Spirit are like the wind. "You can hear the sound of it, but cannot tell where it comes from and where it goes." Mystified, Nicodemus presses Him: "How can these things be?" "If I have told you earthly things and you do not believe, how will you believe if I tell you heavenly things?"

He goes on to explain that God sends His Son into the world out of love, granting to all who believe everlasting life. He comes not to condemn the world but to save a world already condemned, so that it should not perish in darkness, without recourse. As a light shining in an otherwise dark world, the Son draws to Himself all who seek truth while those who love the concealment of darkness "because their deeds were evil" shrink from exposure. "Everyone practicing evil hates the light," Jesus tells him.

12   JERUSALEM TO JUDEA

John's Ministry Eclipsed

◄ John 3:22-36

After the Passover, Jesus travels northward to Samaria with His disciples, preaching and baptizing in the area of Judea. John the Baptist is ministering near Aenon and his disciples become alarmed that people are being drawn away from John to Jesus. "Rabbi," they say, "He who was with you beyond the Jordan, to whom you have testified—behold, He is baptizing, and all are coming to Him!"

John reminds his disciples of his own testimony that "I am not the Christ." He tells them that as Jesus' ministry increases, his own must decrease and likens himself by illustration to a friend of the bridegroom who, while he does not himself possess the bride, "rejoices greatly," sharing the joy of the occasion with Him. "The Father loves the Son," John tells them. It is His Father who has "given all things into His hand."

13   JUDEA TO SYCHAR IN SAMARIA

Departure From Judea

◄ Matthew 4:12
◄ Mark 1:14
◄ Luke 3:19-20, 4:14
◄ John 4:1-4

The Pharisees try to use the success of Jesus' ministry to create a rift between John and Jesus. King Herod has John imprisoned for preaching against his marriage to his brother's wife, Herodias, and against other unsavory things he has done. When Jesus learns that John is in prison, He heads north for Galilee via Sychar in Samaria.

The Woman at the Well

◄ John 4:5-42

It was uncommon during this period for Jews to travel through Samaria because Samaritans were thought to be an impure people. Jesus and His disciples strike out through this region on their way to Galilee and come to the well that the patriarch Jacob built. Here the disciples leave Jesus to rest and head into town to buy food. Eventually a woman arrives in the heat of the day, to draw water from the well. "Give me a drink," Jesus says to her.

"How is it that You, being a Jew, ask a drink from me, a Samaritan woman?" she replies. Jesus tells her that if she knew who was asking, she would ask Him in turn for "living water" that would satisfy her thirst forever. Those who drink the water of this well "will thirst again," Jesus says, "but whoever drinks of the water that I shall give him will never thirst. It will become in him a fountain of water springing up into everlasting life."

"Sir, give me this water, that I may not thirst, nor come here to draw," the woman replies. "Go call your husband and come here," Jesus tells her. "I have no husband," she answers. "You have well said 'I have no husband,'" Jesus says, "for you have had five husbands, and the one whom you now have is not your husband."

"Sir, I perceive that You are a prophet," the woman replies, before turning the conversation to a point of religious dispute between Jews and Samaritans. "Our fathers worshiped on this mountain," she says "and you Jews say that in Jerusalem is the true place where one ought to worship."

"Woman, believe Me," Jesus answers, "the hour is coming when you will neither on this mountain nor in Jerusalem, worship the Father." In that hour, just as God is Spirit, true worshippers will worship Him "in spirit and in truth." The woman professes her belief that when the Messiah comes "He will tell us all things." "I who speak to you am He," Jesus says.

Upon their return, the disciples are surprised to find Jesus talking with the woman and urge Him to partake of the food they have purchased in town. "My food is to do the will of Him who sent me and to finish His work," Jesus says.

"Do you not say, 'There are still four months and then comes the harvest?'" He asks them. "Behold, I say to you, lift up your eyes and look at the fields, for they are already white for harvest!" As the townspeople arrive they urge Him to stay, having been told by the woman to "come, see a man who told me all things that I ever did." She has provoked them asking, "Could this be the Christ?"

Over the course of the next two days many of the Samaritan townspeople come to believe. "Now we believe, not because of what you said," they say to the woman. "For we ourselves have heard Him and we know that this is indeed the Christ, the Savior of the world."

14 SYCHAR TO GALILEE

John 4:43-45 ▶

Jesus in Galilee

Jesus departs, continuing north through Samaria until His arrival in Galilee. The Galileans receive Him because of the events they have witnessed while in Jerusalem at the recent feast.

Conclusion

We examined in this chapter the ministry of John the Baptist, his baptism of Jesus and Jesus' subsequent temptation in the wilderness. We are introduced here to Jesus' ministry, the calling of His first disciples, and His first miracle. We have examined Jesus' trip to Jerusalem, His cleansing of the Temple there, His nocturnal encounter with the Pharisee Nicodemus, and His ministry to the woman at the well.

The Great Galilean Ministry

This chapter contains the Galilean ministry and is full of events that demonstrate Jesus' authority. There is self-disclosure by both word and deed establishing His identity with the Messiah foretold by Scripture.

Summer, A.D. 27

Teaching in Galilee

At 30 years of age Jesus commences His ministry. Luke writes that He returns to Galilee in "the power of the Spirit" teaching, "Repent, for the kingdom of heaven is at hand." He instructs the people in the synagogues and wherever else they happen to gather. The Galileans respond favorably to His message. Reports from Jerusalem create a positive setting for His ministry in Galilee. The signs and wonders at His baptism, the miracle of water turned to wine, the cleansing of the Temple, and His early miracles in Samaria and Galilee have become conspicuous indicators of His messianic identity and mission.

◄ Matthew 4:17
◄ Mark 1:14-15
◄ Luke 4:14-15

15   GALILEE TO CANA

Healing the Nobleman's Son

◄ John 4:46-54

As Jesus makes His way to Nazareth, He travels through Cana, where He recently turned water into wine. Here He encounters a high official who lives in Capernaum but has come some 25 miles to Cana in search of Him. The man's son is gravely ill. Like Nicodemus, the nobleman realizes that Jesus' power is divine in origin, and implores Him to come and heal his son. "Unless you people see signs and wonders you will by no means believe," Jesus answers. The man is undeterred, urging Jesus to "come down before my child dies." "Go your way," Jesus says to him, "your son lives."

The nobleman's servant meets him returning to Capernaum with the good news. "Your son lives!" he says to his master. "Yesterday at the seventh hour the fever left him." The nobleman realizes that his son was healed the moment Jesus said he would live. Compelled by this confirmed display of miraculous power, he and his entire household come to believe. Jesus concludes His ministry here and heads south about ten miles to His hometown, Nazareth.

16   CANA TO NAZARETH

Luke 4:16-30 ▶

First Rejection at Nazareth

In Nazareth, Jesus attends the synagogue on the Sabbath, as is His custom. Here He stands and is handed the scroll of the prophet Isaiah. From a messianic passage in the 61st chapter (see Isaiah 61:1-2), He reads aloud:

> The Spirit of the Lord is upon Me,
> Because He has anointed Me
> To preach the gospel to the poor;
> He has sent Me to heal the brokenhearted,
> To proclaim liberty to the captives
> And recovery of sight to the blind,
> To set at liberty those who are oppressed;
> To proclaim the acceptable year of the Lord.

He then closes the book, hands it back to the attendant and sits down with "the eyes of all who were in the synagogue fixed on him."

In the hush He declares to the assembly: "Today this Scripture is fulfilled in your hearing." Luke tells us that the people marvel at the graciousness of Jesus' words and presence but are bewildered. As His friends and neighbors they know Him only as the son of the carpenter Joseph and his wife Mary, not as the Messiah. Perhaps some of the older folk assembled remember especially the questionable circumstances of Mary's pregnancy and the rather strange events surrounding Jesus' birth. Jesus tells them that while they will expect Him to prove He is the Messiah by signs and wonders, they will receive no such proof since "no prophet is accepted in his own country."

Luke writes that "all those in the synagogue, when they heard these things, were filled with wrath and rose up and thrust Him out of the city." From the brow of the hill on which the city of Nazareth is built they mean to hurl Him over the cliff to His death for arrogance and blasphemy. But Jesus "passing through the midst of them" goes on His way to Capernaum.

17   NAZARETH TO CAPERNAUM

Matthew 4:13-16 ▶

New Home in Capernaum

Jesus' ministry now moves to Capernaum, on the northern coast of the Sea of Galilee, also called the Sea of Tiberias. Although it is located in the land of the Israelite tribes of Zebulun and Naphtali, Capernaum is more Gentile than Jewish. The city exists on the route from Egypt to Damascus, and is inhabited by merchants from all over the world. Matthew sees the location of Jesus' ministry in Capernaum as a fulfillment of the prophecy in Isaiah that Zebulun and Naphtali "have seen a great light," illuminating "the land of the shadow of death" (Isaiah 9:1-2). This city is the home to the fishermen Andrew, Peter, James, and John who figure so significantly in the events which follow.

Calling of the First Four Disciples

As Jesus gains popularity in Capernaum, masses of people gather to hear the Word of God. While He is teaching one day on the seashore where Peter, James, and John are washing their nets, Jesus boards Peter's boat and asks him to push off from shore so that He can minister to the people from a little way out.

◀ Matthew 4:18-22
◀ Mark 1:16-20
◀ Luke 5:1-11

When He finishes speaking to the crowds, Jesus tells Peter to steer for deeper water and let down the nets. Peter protests that he and his partners have been fishing all night and caught nothing, but does as Jesus instructs. A large catch of fish suddenly fills the nets to bursting. As the nets begin to rip apart Peter calls to his partners for help. Their boats are soon so full of fish they founder. Awed by this sudden, stunning reversal of the night's fishing prospects and Jesus' display of power, Peter turns to Him and says, "Depart from me, Lord, for I am a sinful man." "Do not be afraid," Jesus tells him.

"From now on you will catch men," Jesus says to Peter and his companions. Although James, John, Andrew, and Peter already know Jesus, it is at this moment that they leave everything to follow Him, becoming an integral part of His work.

The miraculous catch of fish must have created a great stir in the local fishing industry as well as in the city of Capernaum. It is a first dramatic sign of Jesus' divine authority over the natural world.

Exorcism in the Synagogue

Mark indicates that Jesus' teaching in the synagogue on the following Sabbath has a profound effect on the assembled people. Here He instructs them with authority, expounding the Scriptures with clarity and truth. The signs and miracles that accompany His teaching further authenticate His witness.

◀ Mark 1:21-28
◀ Luke 4:31-37

As He is teaching in the synagogue, a man with an unclean or demonic spirit cries out. "Let us alone! What have we to do with You, Jesus of Nazareth? Did You come to destroy us? I know who You are—the Holy One of God!" Jesus commands the evil spirit to hold its peace and come out of the man so that with a great convulsion and a final cry the spirit is decisively expelled. The people marvel at this demonstration of power. "What a word this is!" they exclaim. "For with authority and power He commands even the unclean spirits and they come out." Jesus' fame accordingly spreads throughout the region around Galilee.

Healing Peter's Mother-in-Law

Matthew 8:14-17 ▶
Mark 1:29-34 ▶
Luke 4:38-41 ▶

After the Sabbath service, Jesus and His followers enter Peter's house where Peter's mother-in-law lies sick. At the behest of His disciples Jesus takes her by the hand and rebukes the fever. By evening, word of the healing is out and the whole city crowds at Peter's door, bringing all those in need of healing. Jesus heals those afflicted by sickness and disease, and casts out many evil spirits, forbidding the demons to reveal His divine identity to the people. In recounting this event, Matthew cites a prophecy fulfilled by Jesus' ministry of healing: "He himself took our infirmities and bore our sicknesses" (see Isaiah 53:4).

18 CAPERNAUM TO GALILEE AND BACK

First Galilean Tour

Matthew 4:23-25 ▶
Mark 1:35-39 ▶
Luke 4:42-44 ▶

The following morning, Jesus heads out long before daylight to spend time alone with God in prayer. When His followers find Him they tell Him the crowds are looking for Him. Jesus replies that they must go to still other towns and villages to preach. He then departs Capernaum to minister with the four fishermen who are His disciples.

His new status as healer and exorcist is confirmed as He travels throughout Galilee, preaching the good news of the Kingdom of God in the synagogues. Everywhere He goes, His message is attested by signs and miracles since "they brought to Him all sick people who were afflicted with various diseases and torments, and those who were demon-possessed, epileptics, and paralytics; and He healed them." News of this ministry spreads throughout Galilee, the Decapolis, Jerusalem, and Judea. The people are so astonished by Jesus that multitudes from various cities begin to follow Him from place to place.

Healing of the Leper

Matthew 8:2-4 ▶
Mark 1:40-45 ▶
Luke 5:12-16 ▶

In one city, Jesus encounters a leper who, kneeling before Him, says, "If You are willing, You can make me clean." Mark reports that Jesus, moved with compassion, replies, "I am willing; be cleansed." Immediately the leprosy is healed, and Jesus instructs the man to tell no one, but to show himself to the priests in Jerusalem and to offer the gift that is commanded in the Law (see Leviticus 14:1-32).

Leprosy was perhaps the most dreaded disease of Jesus' day and the life of a leper was that of a social outcast. Direct contact with a leper was prohibited. Simply touching a leper would cause a person to become ritually unclean for a time, and lepers were not permitted to enter the Temple. The physical defilement of leprosy was closely connected to spiritual defilement, or sin. One of the expectations of the Messiah was that He would be able to heal this defilement, in both its physical and spiritual dimensions.

Spurning the stigma and ritual proscriptions Jesus touches the leper. He then sends the man to the priests as a sign to them that their Messiah has come. This is significant, because the priests must now judge for themselves whether Jesus is in fact the promised Messiah or a false prophet, and guide the people accordingly. The man Jesus cleansed is so elated that he tells his story everywhere he goes.

Healing of the Paralytic

◄ Matthew 9:1-8
◄ Mark 2:1-12
◄ Luke 5:17-26

Jesus then returns to Capernaum by boat. When the people learn that He is back they crowd into the house where He is staying. Among the crowd are Pharisees, teachers of the Law, and religious leaders from Jerusalem who have come to further evaluate the evidence of Jesus' miracles. The leadership may well have come from Jerusalem after hearing the witness of the cleansed leper. Jesus now provides them unmistakable evidence of His authority to heal physical disease and restore spiritual health as well.

Four men with a paralytic friend bring the man to Jesus but cannot find a way in because of the crowd. The resourceful friends remove part of the roof and lower the paralytic into the house. "Son, be of good cheer; your sins are forgiven you," Jesus says to the paralyzed man. The religious leaders present are offended that in making this statement Jesus is presumptuously equating Himself with God, since only God can forgive sins.

Sensing their unrest Jesus asks them: "Which is easier, to say 'Your sins are forgiven you,' or to say, 'Rise up and walk'?" He then demonstrates His authority on earth to forgive sins by telling the man to "Arise, take up your bed, and go to your house." When the man actually stands and walks out of the house carrying his bed and praising God, the crowd is astounded. Jesus' challengers are silenced.

Calling of Matthew (Levi)

◄ Matthew 9:9-13
◄ Mark 2:13-17
◄ Luke 5:27-32

When Jesus leaves the house, He teaches the crowds that follow Him as He walks along the seaside. At one point He passes a man named Levi, or Matthew, who sits collecting taxes, and says to him, "Follow Me." Matthew obeys instantly and later holds a feast for Jesus, inviting all of his friends. The Pharisees, who continue to examine Jesus and His claims, are upset when they see Jesus feasting and enjoying Himself among hated tax collectors and others with whom they refuse to associate. "Why does your Teacher eat with tax collectors and sinners?" the Pharisees ask the disciples. "Those who are well have no need of a physician, but those who are sick," Jesus answers. This feast takes place about one year into Jesus' public ministry.

John's Disciples Question Jesus

◄ Matthew 9:14-17
◄ Mark 2:18-22
◄ Luke 5:33-39

When the disciples of John the Baptist approach Jesus to ask why His disciples do not keep the tradition of fasting while they and the Pharisees do. Jesus answers with three analogies:

● He likens Himself to a groom among his guests at a wedding. With the bridegroom present, it is a time for feasting rather than fasting. A time will come when fasting is appropriate.

● If you try to patch an old garment using a new and unshrunken piece of cloth, the tear will only become worse.

● If you put new wine into old wineskins, the fermentation of the new wine will cause the skins to burst, and both the wine and the skins will be lost.

Although Jesus does not come to abolish the Law or the Prophets, it is also clear that His teaching overturns many of the traditions and mis-interpretations of the Law and the Prophets that the Pharisees and others practiced and taught. Many of the traditions of the Pharisees must be discarded or reformed if they are to receive the New Covenant Jesus has come to inaugurate.

Conclusion
We have seen in this chapter a terrific display of Jesus' power over the demonic world, disease, and nature—things over which people are ordinarily powerless.

The Beginning of the Opposition and the Sermon on the Mount

The Gospel writers have confronted us with prodigious evidence for why they, and many of the people, have come to believe that Jesus is the Messiah. The religious leaders have thus far said very little. When Jesus sends the cleansed leper to them, they are forced to address the question of Jesus' amply demonstrated power.

Previously we have seen the leadership upset by His claim of authority to forgive sin and by His association with a hated tax collector, Levi. In the coming chapters we will see their opposition stiffen as they continue to examine His words and deeds. They fail to comprehend why He resists conforming to their rigid traditions of Sabbath-keeping, and will eventually take issue with other areas of His teaching and work.

Spring, A.D. 28

19 CAPERNAUM TO JERUSALEM

The Pool of Bethesda

◀ John 5:1-47

In the spring Jesus returns to Jerusalem for what is likely the feast of Passover. About a year has passed since His last visit to the city, recorded in the second chapter of John.

In Jerusalem Jesus visits the Pool of Bethesda with its five porticoes where a multitude of "sick people, blind, lame, [and] paralyzed" gather each year waiting for "the moving of the water." It is believed "an angel went down at a certain time into the pool and stirred up the water" and that whoever stepped in first would be healed.

Jesus approaches a particularly desperate man suffering an infirmity which prevents him from lowering himself into the pool in time to receive healing. "Sir," the man tells Jesus, "I have no man to put me into the pool when the water is stirred up; but while I am coming another steps down before me." John writes that the man had suffered thus some 38 years. "Rise, take up your bed and walk," Jesus says. The lame man is instantly healed and does as he is commanded. When the Jewish religious leaders in Jerusalem see the man carrying his bed on the Sabbath day they are scandalized and reprove him accordingly. "It is not lawful for you to carry your bed," they tell him. It constitutes a violation of the Sabbath laws. Though a man so restored is a testimony of divine power, this fact is ignored by the leaders who begin plotting to kill Jesus after identifying Him as the healer.

Jesus' opponents are further antagonized by His addressing God as Father since by so doing He is understood to be equating Himself with God. But this is surely the least of their worries where Jesus' statements about Himself are concerned, since He claims His Father grants Him authority to execute judgment and with it power to raise the dead. "The hour is coming," Jesus tells them, when "all who are in their graves" will hear My voice and "come forth to the resurrection of life" or "to the resurrection of condemnation" according to their deeds. He assures them that anyone who "receives Him" has everlasting life and "shall not come into judgment" but has passed "from death to life."

Jesus allows that if He were bearing witness to Himself by improbable claims to divine authority, His testimony would scarcely be credible and could justly be ignored. But as it is His words are attested by the miraculous nature of His works among them and foretold by the Law of Moses, which they profess to hold sacred. He warns them that Moses, whom they claim to believe, will himself accuse them before God since it is of Jesus that Moses wrote in messianic anticipation of His coming.

20 FROM JERUSALEM TO A WHEATFIELD ON THE WAY TO GALILEE

Matthew 12:1-8 ▶
Mark 2:23-28 ▶
Luke 6:1-5 ▶

Wheatfield Controversy

On their departure from Jerusalem, Jesus and His disciples provoke the second in a series of Sabbath controversies. His disciples are found plucking heads of grain to eat as they walk through the fields in Galilee on the Sabbath. Pharisees ask Jesus why He allows His followers to do what they consider unlawful on the Sabbath, and Jesus replies with two examples from Scripture that demonstrate the nature of God's commandments.

"Have you never read what David did when he was in need and hungry?" Jesus inquires of the Pharisees. He is referring here to 1 Samuel 21:1-6, where the high priest allows David and his men who are fleeing the wrath of King Saul to have the showbread that is reserved by law for the high priest alone. By this first example Jesus argues that the laws governing Sabbath observance are not as rigidly inviolable as the Pharisees teach. Given the fugitives' lack of provisions, the case of David and the showbread constitutes a permissible exception on the basis of mercy.

In the second case Jesus cites the laws prescribing the work of Temple priests and Levites on the Sabbath (see Numbers 28:9-10). It is certainly no secret to the Pharisees challenging Jesus that the work of the priests actually increases on the Sabbath, extending to include additional Sabbath burnt offerings and libations. The priests are routinely exempted from Sabbath rest to fulfill their role as priests. In their zeal to enforce the letter of the law the Pharisees miss the spirit of mercy and good sense that should decide its application.

In His refutation of their unmerciful legalism Jesus cites the prophet Hosea and God's reproval of His people: "For I desire mercy and not sacrifice" (Hosea 6:6). "If you had known what this means," Jesus says, "you would not have condemned the guiltless…The Sabbath was made for man, not man for the Sabbath." Finally, that His followers pluck grain to eat is really no great matter since "the Son of Man is Lord even of the Sabbath." These examples from Scripture demonstrate Jesus' authority to interpret the commandments and teach that God has given them not to burden people, but to bless them.

21 FROM A WHEATFIELD TO A SYNAGOGUE IN GALILEE

Healing of the Withered Hand

Jesus provokes a third Sabbath controversy when He heals a man with a withered hand in a synagogue. Anticipating the objections of those looking for grounds to accuse Him of violating the Sabbath, Jesus calls for the crippled man to "arise and stand here" in their midst.

◀ Matthew 12:9-14
◀ Mark 3:1-6
◀ Luke 6:6-11

"What man is there among you who has one sheep, and if it falls into a pit on the Sabbath, will not lay hold of it and lift it out?" Jesus asks. "Of how much more value is a man than a sheep? . . . Is it lawful on the Sabbath to do good or to do evil?"

In response to these trenchant questions His detractors remain obstinately silent. Jesus looks "around at them with anger, being grieved by the hardness of their hearts" and then commands the crippled man to "stretch out your hand." The withered hand is immediately restored "as whole as the other" and the Pharisees, filled with rage, depart the synagogue plotting to destroy Him.

In these three Sabbath controversies, the charges against Jesus that He is violating the Sabbath commandment are unfounded. Jesus refutes the religious leaders' merciless and hypocritical Sabbath traditions so decisively that they are provoked to kill Him for the threat He represents to their authority.

22   THE SYNAGOGUE TO THE SEA OF GALILEE

Matthew 12:15-21 ▶
Mark 3:7-12 ▶

Withdrawal to the Seashore

Aware of the plots being formed against Him, Jesus and His disciples depart the synagogue and go down to the shore at the Sea of Galilee. People flock to them from Galilee, Judea, Jerusalem, Idumea, Tyre, Sidon, and "beyond the Jordan." The crowds are so great Jesus tells His disciples a small boat must be "kept ready for Him because of the multitude, lest they should crush Him." Here Jesus continues His ministry to the great multitudes, healing the sick and casting out demons. Just as in the case of the man at the Galilean synagogue the demonic spirits recognize Jesus and fall down before him crying, "You are the Son of God." Jesus forbids them to proclaim Him just as He enjoins the many people healed not to make Him known. This is to fulfill the words of the prophet Isaiah who writes of the Messiah:

> Behold! My Servant whom I uphold, My Elect One in whom My soul delights! I have put My Spirit upon Him; He will bring forth justice to the Gentiles. He will not cry out, nor raise His voice, Nor cause His voice to be heard in the street. A bruised reed He will not break, and smoking flax He will not quench; He will bring forth justice for truth. He will not fail nor be discouraged, Till He has established justice in the earth.   — Isaiah 42:1-4

23   FROM THE SEA OF GALILEE TO A MOUNTAIN NEAR CAPERNAUM

Summer, A.D. 28

Mark 3:13-19 ▶
Luke 6:12-16 ▶

Appointment of the Twelve Apostles

Later Jesus withdraws from the multitudes and spends a night alone in prayer on a mountain in a range near the Sea of Galilee. The next morning He calls His disciples together and from them selects twelve to be His apostles. A *disciple* is merely a *learner* or *follower*, while the term *apostle* means *one who is sent*. The selection of twelve "to be with Him and that He might send them out to preach" is a significant turning point in Jesus' public ministry. Until this time we find Jesus ministering mainly to the crowds that gather spontaneously. He now appoints twelve to be with Him in a special relationship of training and instruction. The focus of Jesus' ministry begins to shift from the masses to these few men whom He will prepare and send out to teach on His behalf.

Sermon on the Mount

◄ Matthew 5:1–8:1
◄ Luke 6:17-49

After His selection of the Twelve, Jesus delivers His most famous sermon seated on a mountain with His diciples and the people gathered around Him. He begins by announcing the coming of the messianic kingdom in a series of blessings also known as the Beatitudes. Jesus calls His listeners to a life of righteousness, then expounds for them the true meaning of the term. The key verse in His exposition is Matthew 5:17—"Do not think that I came to destroy the Law or the Prophets. I did not come to destroy but to fulfill."

Standing in a relationship of perfect obedience to the commandments of God, Jesus urges the people to a devout observance that exceeds the legalistic applications so prevalent among the Jewish religious leadership. For instance, while the Law states, "Thou shall not commit adultery," the adulterous thought is itself a sin, one tantamount to the crime. Likewise, injurious thoughts and feelings toward another person are sinful even if they are not acted out. He teaches that love and mercy are the true foundation of the commandments.

Jesus uses the examples of almsgiving, prayer, and fasting to demonstrate His point. Although these are good things to do, if they are done in the wrong spirit they become self-serving rather than glorifying to God. If we obey the commandments so as to appear righteous we defeat God's purpose in giving them.

God's will for us is that we walk in the freedom of obedience to Him, letting our light "so shine before men" that they see our good works and glorify Him. It is here Jesus first gives the Lord's Prayer as instruction on how to pray.

He teaches that God is concerned not just with our outward actions, but with our inner intentions as well. He teaches our motivation should be for God and His kingdom, rather than for ourselves and our own kingdoms on earth. Jesus urges His followers that if they will be single-minded toward God, they will not need to worry about material things like food, clothing and shelter, because God will provide these things for them.

There is a shift in focus from the temporal to the eternal, and from the external to the internal. We must not be preoccupied with other people and their faults. "Judge not, that you be not judged," Jesus tells the people. We are to be responsible for our own shortcomings, leaving the judgment of others to God and demonstrating mercy toward one another, since if we do not forgive others neither will God forgive us. Jesus summarizes the Law and the Prophets in the Golden Rule: "Whatever you want men to do to you, do also to them."

In conclusion, Jesus warns His listeners about the difficulty of the path of true righteousness. He cautions them against hypocrisy and disobedience. Merely calling Him "Lord" does not make one a true follower. He reasserts His claim to messianic authority, equating obedience to His words with obedience to God. When He is finished, His audience is "astonished at His teaching" since He teaches them "as one having authority, and not as the scribes."

Conclusion

In this chapter we see Jesus reject the legalistic and hypocritical interpretation of Scripture promulgated by the Pharisees and argue before the people a vision of holiness based on a faithful representation of scriptural truth. He selects twelve men to train for the remainder of His ministry.

Frontal Attack by Enemies Followed by Parables of the Kingdom

In this chapter the religious leaders categorically reject Jesus and His works. They decide that His power to heal is demonic in origin. We see important changes in Jesus' ministry as He begins to evade the masses and to give Himself to the training of the Twelve. He teaches in parables, concealing their meanings from the crowds and explaining them to His disciples privately.

Summer, A.D. 28

24   FROM A MOUNTAIN NEAR CAPERNAUM BACK TO CAPERNAUM

◀ Matthew 8:5-13
◀ Luke 7:1-10

Healing of the Centurion's Servant

After the Sermon on the Mount, Jesus makes His way back to Capernaum. On entering town a Roman centurion meets Him and says, "Lord, my servant is lying at home paralyzed, dreadfully tormented." Jesus agrees to accompany the centurion: "I will come and heal him," He says. The centurion asks Him instead to simply give the command. "Lord, I am not worthy that You should come under my roof. But only speak the word and my servant shall be healed."

Jesus marvels that the faith of the Gentile soldier is unmatched "even in Israel." He warns His followers that "many will come from east and west, and sit down with Abraham, Isaac, and Jacob in the kingdom of heaven" while "the sons of the kingdom will be cast out." By this statement He indicates the incorporation of righteous Gentiles among the faithful and the exclusion of those relying merely on Jewish ancestry to save them.

The Hebrew Scriptures testify repeatedly that the kingdom of God will be comprised of both Jew and Gentile. As early as the promise to Abraham, assurance is given that "all the families of the earth shall be blessed" (Genesis 12:3). Later the Psalmist will call for "the redeemed of the Lord" whom He has "gathered out of the lands from the east and from the west, from the north and from the south" to declare their redemption by God (Psalm 107:2-3).

In the Book of Isaiah we read that the Messiah will "restore the preserved ones of Israel" and appear "as a light to the Gentiles," heralding "salvation to the ends of the earth" (Isaiah 49:6). These and numerous other prophecies prefigure and proclaim the universal scope of God's love and redemption (See also Amos 9:11-12; Isaiah 1:10; 45:23; 65:1-2; Deuteronomy 32:31; Hosea 1:10; 2:23; Psalm 18:43-44; Joel 2:28-29). The healing of the centurion's servant is the first instance in the Gospels of the inclusion of Gentiles in Jesus' ministry.

25 CAPERNAUM TO NAIN AND THE SURROUNDING REGION

Luke 7:11-17 ▶

The Raising of the Widow's Son at Nain

Soon afterward, Jesus and His disciples, thronged by a large crowd, head south to the city of Nain where they encounter the funeral procession of a young man, "the only son of his mother," herself a widow. When Jesus sees her, He "has compassion on her" and says to her, "Do not weep." He then halts the procession, touching the open coffin and speaking to the corpse: "Young man, I say to you, Arise." To the astonishment of the crowd, the young man sits up and begins talking. Jesus presents him raised from the dead to his mother so that "fear came upon all and they glorified God saying, 'A great prophet has risen up among us' and, 'God has visited His people.'"

Matthew 11:2-19 ▶
Luke 7:18-35 ▶

Eulogy for John the Baptist

Incredible reports like those of the widow's son in Nain soon reach the ears of John the Baptist in his prison cell. While still in the vicinity of Nain Jesus encounters two of John's disciples sent by him to inquire, "Are you the Coming One or do we look for another?"

Jesus instructs John's disciples to "go and tell John the things you have seen and heard: that the blind see, the lame walk, the lepers are cleansed, the deaf hear, the dead are raised, the poor have the gospel preached to them." These were signs that had long been prophesied of the Christ (see Isaiah 29:18-19; 35:5-6; 61:1).

Jesus' eulogy for John confirms that the Baptist is indeed a prophet, "and more than a prophet." He identifies John as "he of whom it is written," the "Elijah" of Malachi (see Malachi 3:1; 4:5). "There has not risen one greater than John the Baptist," Jesus tells the assembled people, "but he who is least in the kingdom of heaven is greater than he."

Those baptized by John rejoice to hear Jesus' authentication of John's ministry, but there are many present, "Pharisees and lawyers," who repudiate both the baptism of John and the messianic teachings of Jesus. Jesus declares that they have thereby "rejected the will of God for themselves," and likens them to children sulking. When their own selfish and obstinate presumptions about who the Messiah would be were disappointed, they became sullen and cantankerous. "John the Baptist came neither eating bread nor drinking wine" and they denounced him saying, "He has a demon," Jesus observes. But when "the Son of Man" comes both "eating and drinking," they say instead, "Look, a glutton and a winebibber, a friend of tax collectors and sinners!"

Judgment on Chorazin, Bethsaida, and Capernaum

◄ Matthew 11:20-30

He then turns His rebuke on the towns where He has performed signs and wonders. He compares Chorazin, Bethsaida, and Capernaum to Tyre, Sidon, and Sodom, three cities judged harshly by God (see Isaiah 23; Genesis 19). "For if the mighty works which were done in you had been done in Tyre and Sidon, they would have repented long ago in sackcloth and ashes," Jesus says. The city of Sodom, destroyed by brimstone and fire from heaven, would itself have "remained until this day" had it been given the same compelling evidence and forewarning to repent. A far greater condemnation awaits those who stubbornly refuse the evidence of divine power in their midst.

Jesus thanks His Father for concealing His message from the "wise and prudent," revealing it instead to "babes." He makes a wide appeal for the people to come to Him since "all things have been delivered to Me by My Father." No one can know the Father except the Son "and the one to whom the Son wills to reveal Him." Jesus bids them, "Come to me, all you who labor and are heavy laden, and I will give you rest." His offer to "take My yoke upon you" is a Hebrew trope for becoming a disciple.

Anointing by the Sinful Woman

◄ Luke 7:36-50

During this period Jesus accepts the invitation of the Pharisee Simon to dine at his house. While there "a woman in the city who was a sinner" enters with "an alabaster flask of fragrant oil," weeping. She begins "to wash His feet with her tears," wiping them "with the hair of her head." She kisses them, anointing them with the fragrant oil. Witnessing this moving display, Simon only reproaches Jesus for allowing a sinner to touch Him, saying to himself, "This Man, if He were a prophet, would know who and what manner of woman this is who is touching Him, for she is a sinner." Jesus, knowing Simon's heart, responds with a parable.

The parable concerns two debtors, one who owes a small amount and one who owes much. Since the lender forgives both men their debts, which one, Jesus asks, will love the lender more? "I suppose the one whom he forgave more," Simon answers. "You have rightly judged," Jesus tells him before turning the parable against Simon's own poor hospitality and ingratitude.

"Do you see this woman?" Jesus asks. "I entered your house; you gave me no water for My feet; but she has washed My feet with her tears, and wiped them with the hair of her head." While Simon has offered no kiss, "this woman has not ceased to kiss My feet since the time I came in." Neither has Simon anointed His head with oil as the woman has so lavishly anointed His feet. "Therefore I say to you her sins, which are many, are forgiven her," Jesus says, "for she loved much." To the woman He addresses words of absolution: "Your sins are forgiven. Your faith has saved you. Go in peace." The dinner guests marvel at Jesus' exercise of a divine prerogative, saying to themselves, "Who is this who even forgives sins?"

26 THE REGION OF NAIN TO THE 2ND GALILEAN PREACHING TOUR

Fall, A.D. 28

Luke 8:1-3 ▶

Second Galilean Tour

Jesus commences a second tour of the Galilean countryside. He continues to announce the coming of the kingdom of God throughout the cities and villages. His twelve disciples accompany Him, as do Mary Magdalene, Joanna the wife of King Herod's steward, Susanna, and many others who support His ministry.

Matthew 12:22-37 ▶
Mark 3:19-30 ▶

Exorcism and Blasphemous Accusations

In Galilee again, Jesus enters a house and there exorcises a man "demon possessed, blind and mute." He is immediately accused by the Pharisees and scribes of doing so by the power of Beelzebub, the prince of demons. This encounter with the religious leaders will have a major repercussion on Jesus' ministry because the people look to these leaders for guidance about the legitimacy of any messianic claim. Having just witnessed a miracle performed by the power of God, the Pharisees for the first time render their public verdict: Jesus is the agent of Satan rather than their Messiah.

Jesus responds by pointing out that if Satan casts out Satan, his kingdom cannot stand, and asks His opponents by what power their own followers cast out demons. He warns against the blasphemy of the Holy Spirit (the "unpardonable sin"): Though witnesses to the good work of the Holy Spirit, they spitefully attribute that work to Satan. He warns them that they will be judged for their words since it is "out of the abundance of the heart [that] the mouth speaks…[and] for every idle word men may speak, they will give account of it in the day of judgment."

Matthew 12:38-45 ▶

The Pharisees Demand a Sign

While still in the house certain of the scribes and Pharisees cajole Jesus: "Teacher, we want to see a sign from You." Jesus refuses, describing them as "an evil and adulterous generation." He warns them that the only sign given them will be "the sign of the prophet Jonah," who spent three days in the belly of a large fish before preaching at the city of Nineveh. This is figurative language foretelling that He will be three days in the "belly" of the earth before His resurrection from the dead. The Gentile citizens of Nineveh will rise up one day in condemnation of them. They repented when Jonah preached, where "this genera-tion" repudiates the testimony of one greater than the prophet Jonah.

Joining this condemnation will be "the queen of the South." Jesus is referring here to a visit paid by the Queen of Sheba to Jerusalem dur-ing the reign of King Solomon. She will add her denunciation to that of the Ninevites, because she traveled a great distance to hear wisdom about the God of Israel from Solomon, where they have refused one greater than Solomon teaching in their midst.

Finally, He compares them to a man from whom a demon departs but whose house remains vacant, unfilled by God's Spirit. The demon re-turns and, finding the house "empty, swept, and put in order" but still untenanted, recruits "seven other spirits more wicked than himself" to inhabit it with him. The man ends in worse shape than before the demon departed. Jesus warns His opponents by this analogy that their refusal to accept Him will mean a worse fate for them than if they had never served God in the first place.

The Concerns of Jesus' Family

◄ Matthew 12:46-50
◄ Mark 3:31-35
◄ Luke 8:19-21

Having heard perhaps of the Pharisees' public renunciation of Jesus, His family comes looking for Him. Getting word that His mother and brothers desire to speak with Him but are prevented by the crowds blocking entrance to the house, Jesus addresses a question to the people, "Who is My mother and who are My brothers?" He then answers the question: "Whoever does the will of My Father in heaven is My brother and sister and mother." Later Jesus departs the house and goes down to the Sea of Galilee.

27 FROM A HOUSE IN GALILEE TO THE SEA OF GALILEE

Teaching by Parables

◄ Matthew 13:1-53
◄ Mark 4:1-34
◄ Luke 8:4-18

Here Jesus begins to teach the people in parables. The shift to this manner of teaching excludes many of the people by concealing Jesus' meaning in figures. It is foretold by the Psalmist who writes "I will open my mouth in parables; I will utter things kept secret from the foundation of the world" (Psalm 78:2). By this method Jesus focuses His attention on the apostles and others who have "ears to hear." From a boat on the Sea of Galilee He delivers:

● The parable of the sower and the seed, in which the seed represents the Word of God, the sower, the one who carries the message. The field in which the seed falls represents the different responses people make to God's Word.

● The parable of the seed growing of itself, in which the kingdom of God is likened to a seed whose growth is mysterious.

THE LIFE OF CHRIST

- The parable of the wheat and the tares, in which the souls of men and women are compared to wheat and tares. The righteous souls (wheat) and the unrighteous (tares) will coexist until the final judgment, when they will be separated.

- The parable of the mustard seed, in which the kingdom of God is likened to a tiny seed that grows into a massive tree.

- The parable of the leaven, in which the growth of God's kingdom in the world is compared to leaven that eventually permeates the entire lump of dough.

28 THE SEA OF GALILEE TO THE DISCIPLE'S HOUSE

Jesus then leaves the multitudes and enters a house with His disciples. He explains to them the meaning of the parable of the wheat and the tares and then delivers another series of parables:

- The parable of the hidden treasure, which describes unexpected joy for those who find the kingdom of God.

- The parable of the pearl of great price, which depicts the matchless value of the kingdom of God for those who find it.

- The parable of the dragnet, which represents the separation of saints and sinners on the day of judgment.

"Have you understood all of these things?" Jesus asks His disciples. "Yes, Lord," they reply. "Therefore every scribe instructed concerning the kingdom of heaven is like a householder who brings out of his treasure things new and old," Jesus says.

29 THE DISCIPLE'S HOUSE TO THE REGION OF THE GERASENES

Calming of the Storm

Matthew 8:18, 23-27 ▶
Mark 4:35-41 ▶
Luke 8:22-25 ▶

When evening comes Jesus, accompanied by His disciples, sets out in a boat for the region of the Gerasenes, on the southeastern shore of the Sea of Galilee, and then falls asleep on a cushion as they sail. "Suddenly a great tempest arose on the sea," and the waves begin to beat against and flood the boat. Jesus remains fast asleep. Fearing for their lives, the disciples wake Him crying, "Lord, save us! We are perishing!" Roused from sleep, Jesus rebukes the storm: "Peace, be still!"

46

The wind instantly ceases and there is "a great calm." "Why are you so fearful?" Jesus admonishes His disciples. "How is it that you have no faith?" The disciples marvel, wondering, "Who is this, that even the wind and sea obey him?" The miracle is a private demonstration to His disciples of His messianic authority and power.

Exorcism of the Gerasene Demoniac

◀ Matthew 8:28-34
◀ Mark 5:1-20
◀ Luke 8:26-39

As they arrive at the other side of the sea, a man (or two, per Matthew) "who had demons for a long time" and "wore no clothes" encounters Jesus and His disciples, "coming out of the tombs, exceedingly fierce, so that none could pass that way." The man "had his dwelling among the tombs" and while he had "often been bound with shackles and chains" he only pulled them apart or broke them in pieces, running wild in the mountains, crying and "cutting himself with stones." The demon possessing the man recognizes Jesus and cries out, "What have we to do with You, Jesus, You Son of God? Have you come here to torment us before the time?"

"What is your name?" Jesus asks the spirit. "Legion," the demon replies, "for we are many." The demons beg Jesus not to force them "out into the abyss," but into a herd of swine feeding on the mountains, instead. "If you cast us out," they implore Him, "send us to the swine, that we may enter them." Jesus grants them their request and the demons enter the swine. The herd of about two thousand charges "violently down the steep place into the sea." At this the swineherds flee the scene and report the event in the city.

Residents of the city come out to investigate. Finding the formerly possessed man "clothed and in his right mind," they are filled with fear and urge Jesus to leave. The man who has been delivered asks Jesus for leave to accompany Him. Jesus commands him instead to "go home to your friends, and tell them what great things the Lord has done for you, and how He has had compassion on you."

30 THE REGION OF THE GERASENES TO CAPERNAUM

Healing of Jairus' Daughter

◀ Matthew 9:18-26
◀ Mark 5:21-43
◀ Luke 8:40-56

He then returns by boat to Capernaum on the other side of the sea, where He is met again by the crowds. Here a synagogue official named Jairus "fell down at Jesus' feet," entreating him: "My little daughter lies at the point of death. Come and lay Your hands on her." Jairus' child is an "only daughter about twelve years of age" and Jesus consents to come, "but as He went the multitudes thronged Him."

On the way to the official's house, a woman with "a flow of blood" who has unavailingly spent "all her livelihood on physicians" touches the hem of Jesus' garment, believing that if she but touches Him she will be

47

made well. Sensing that power has gone out from Him, Jesus turns to ask who touched Him. The woman "fearing and trembling" confesses that she was healed the instant she made contact. "Be of good cheer daughter," Jesus says to her, "your faith has made you well."

At this point someone from the official's house meets them and says to Jairus, "Your daughter is dead. Why trouble the Teacher further?" Jesus tells Jairus not to be afraid, "only believe, and she will be made well." Arriving at the house, Jesus "saw a tumult and those who wept and wailed loudly."

"Why make this commotion and weep?" He asks. "The child is not dead but sleeping." The mourners only ridicule Him, "knowing that she was dead," but Jesus "put them all outside" and entering the house allows no one to accompany Him "except Peter, James, and John, and the father and mother of the girl."

"Little girl," Jesus says, "arise." The girl stands and walks around, and Jesus commands that something be given her to eat. The people in the house who only moments earlier were mourning the girl's death are now overcome with amazement and joy.

Healing of Two Blind Men

Matthew 9:27-34 ▶

Later He encounters two blind men crying, "Son of David, Have mercy on us." "Do you believe I am able to do this?" Jesus asks them. "Yes, Lord," they reply. Touching their eyes Jesus says to them, "According to your faith let it be to you." At this the men's eyes are opened and, although He charges them sternly to tell no one, they broadcast the news across the surrounding country.

Jesus then casts a spirit from "a man mute and demon-possessed." The multitudes surrounding him are amazed. "It was never seen like this in Israel!" they enthuse. The Pharisees only malign Him: "He casts out demons by the ruler of demons."

Winter, A.D. 28/29

31 | FROM CAPERNAUM TO THE THIRD TOUR OF GALILEE

Final Rejection in Nazareth

Matthew 13:54-58 ▶
Mark 6:1-6 ▶

As He begins His third tour of Galilee, Jesus returns a final time to His hometown, Nazareth. His teaching in the synagogue on the Sabbath day is so profound that His listeners wonder where He receives such wisdom, and by what power He performs such astonishing miracles.

"Is this not the carpenter, the Son of Mary, and the brother of James, John, Judas, and Simon?" they ask, "And His sisters, are they not all with us? Where then did this Man get all these things?" Jesus tells them that "a prophet is not without honor except in his own country, among his own relatives, and in his own house." Because of their lack of faith He heals only a few sick people here before moving on.

The Mission of the Twelve

◄ Matthew 9:35–11:1
◄ Mark 6:6-13
◄ Luke 9:1-6

Jesus continues through the cities and villages in Galilee, teaching in the synagogues and healing all kinds of illness and disease. He likens the crowds to an abundant harvest with too few reapers, and commands His disciples to pray that workers be sent out into the harvest.

Jesus has been training the twelve disciples, and He now instructs them to go out in pairs to do the work that they have seen Him doing: "And as you go, preach, saying, 'The kingdom of heaven is at hand.' Heal the sick, cleanse the lepers, raise the dead, cast out demons. Freely you have received, freely give." He forbids them to take any money or food or extra clothing with them, directing them instead to stay with worthy people in each town who can accommodate them until they are ready to depart.

He sends the Twelve initially into the towns and cities of Israel, but warns them that they will be arrested and brought before both Jewish and Gentile authorities. "Behold, I send you out as sheep in the midst of wolves," Jesus says, "be wise as serpents and harmless as doves." God will give them the right words to say when they must give an account of themselves but He warns them of the hatred and persecution that their ministry will provoke: "They will deliver you up to councils and scourge you in their synagogues. You will be brought before governors and kings for My sake, as a testimony to them and to the Gentiles."

At these moments they are to trust in God's protection: "Are not two sparrows sold for a copper coin? And not one of them falls to the ground apart from your Fathers will." Therefore "do not fear," He says, "you are of more value than many sparrows."

"Do not think that I came to bring peace on earth," Jesus warns His disciples. "I did not come to bring peace but a sword." Whoever "loves father or mother . . . son or daughter more than Me" or declines "to take his cross and follow after Me is not worthy of Me."

"He who finds his life will lose it," Jesus tells them. But, "He who loses his life for My sake will find it." The disciples are then dispatched in pairs.

Death of John the Baptist

◄ Matthew 14:1-12
◄ Mark 6:14-29
◄ Luke 9:7-9

When King Herod marries his brother Philip's wife, Herodias, John the Baptist antagonizes the king and his new wife by publicly condemning the marriage. "It is not lawful for you to have your brother's wife," he charges. As a result Herod "laid hold of John and bound him, and put him in prison for the sake of Herodias." Mark writes that although Herodias "held it against [John] and wanted to kill him" Herod protects him "for Herod feared John, knowing that he was a just and holy man."

At a feast celebrating his birthday Herod invites "his nobles, the high officers, and the chief men of Galilee." During the party Herodias' daughter dances for the king and so pleases him that he makes an oath to give her whatever she wishes. "Whatever you ask me I will give you, up to half my kingdom," Herod tells the girl. "What shall I ask?" Salome inquires of her mother. At Herodias' urging, the girl returns an answer to Herod and his guests: "I want you to give me at once the head of John the Baptist on a platter," she demands. King Herod reluctantly agrees and "John's head was brought on a platter and given to the girl, and she brought it to her mother." John's disciples come and carry John's body away for burial and then report his death to Jesus. Later, when King Herod hears about Jesus, he is convinced that "this is John, whom I beheaded" and "he has been raised from the dead."

Conclusion

Many of the miracles recorded in this chapter are demonstrations to Jesus' disciples of His true nature. They reflect a shift from the public to a private emphasis in His ministry.

Training of the Twelve in Discipleship

Having been rejected by the religious leadership of Israel, Jesus selects twelve men and begins training them to lead His followers. These leaders are selected not on the basis of ancestral or tribal identity, but for their simple faith in His messianic mission. Jesus' attention will now increasingly turn to their careful instruction.

Spring, A.D. 29

32 THE GALILEAN TOUR TO A WILDERNESS NEAR BETHSAIDA

Debriefing the Twelve and Feeding the 5,000

The apostles return from their missionary work and report all the things they did and taught while away. Jesus bids them to "come aside by yourselves to a deserted place and rest a while." Together they withdraw by boat to a spot near Bethsaida but the crowd races ahead of them on land and arrives before they do on the other side of the sea. It is possible that many of these are followers of John the Baptist, who has just been beheaded. Jesus "is moved with compassion for them." They are "like sheep without a shepherd." He begins to teach them and to heal those who are sick.

As evening draws near, Jesus turns to Philip, "Where shall we buy bread that these may eat?" Philip replies that "two hundred denarii worth of bread is not sufficient for them, that every one of them may have a little." Andrew offers that "there is a lad here who has five barley loaves and two small fish." But "what are they among so many?" he says. Jesus tells them to "make the people sit down." Counting just the men, there are about five thousand present.

Taking the five loaves and two fish, Jesus blesses them and gives the food to His disciples to distribute. The crowd eats "as much as they wanted" and when the meal is over the disciples collect 12 baskets full of food "left over by those who had eaten."

◄ Matthew 14:13-21
◄ Mark 6:30-44
◄ Luke 9:10-17
◄ John 6:1-13

33 FROM THE BETHSAIDA WILDERNESS TO THE PLAIN OF GENNESARET

Attempt to Make Him King

After the meal, Jesus immediately sends His disciples back across the Sea of Galilee to Capernaum while He dismisses the crowd. Those present become convinced that "this is truly the prophet who is to come into the

◄ Matthew 14:22-23
◄ Mark 6:45-46
◄ John 6:14-15

world." The crowd is so impressed by the miracle that they are moved to take Jesus by force and make Him king. Sensing this, Jesus withdraws from them to a mountain and prays in solitude.

Jesus Walks on Water

Matthew 14:24-33 ▶
Mark 6:47-52 ▶
John 6:16-21 ▶

Sometime between three and six in the morning, the boat the disciples are rowing is being "tossed by the waves" about three miles out. They are straining against a contrary wind when Jesus approaches the boat, walking on the sea. "It is a ghost!" the disciples cry. "Be of good cheer!" Jesus assures them. "It is I; do not be afraid." At this Peter says to Him, "Lord, if it is You, command me to come to You on the water." "Come," Jesus says, and Peter, too, walks out onto the surface of the water.

With the boat behind him, Peter takes fright, seeing that "the wind was boisterous." "Lord, save me!" he cries as he begins to sink. Jesus instantly stretches out his hand and catches him. "O you of little faith," Jesus chides, "why did you doubt?" The two then rejoin the astonished disciples in the boat. As soon as they board the wind ceases. Staggered by this latest turn of events, Jesus' disciples bow down before Him. "Truly, you are the Son of God," they confess.

Reception at Gennesaret

Matthew 14:34-36 ▶
Mark 6:53-56 ▶

The boat lands on the Plains of Gennesaret, near Capernaum, and the people there realize quickly who has arrived. The news spreads throughout the area so that "wherever He entered, into villages, cities, or the country" people "laid the sick in the marketplaces, and begged Him that they might just touch the hem of His garment." The power over sickness dispensed by Jesus is so potent that all who touch Him are "made perfectly well."

34 FROM THE GENNESARET PLAIN TO CAPERNAUM

Bread of Life

John 6:22-71 ▶

When the crowd that was fed with the loaves and fish realizes that Jesus has departed, they get into boats and cross the sea in search of Him. The puzzled crowd finds Him in the synagogue and asks how it is He has arrived at Capernaum. They are of course unaware of His miraculous late night crossing of the sea. In response Jesus rebukes them for being motivated by hunger rather than by their more pressing spiritual needs. "Do not labor for the food which perishes," He adjures them, "but for the food which endures to everlasting life."

"What shall we do," the crowd demands, "that we may work the works of God?" Jesus answers that the work of God is to believe in the one whom God sends. The crowd which just yesterday saw the miracle of the loaves and fish now demands from Him a sign. "What sign will

THE LIFE OF CHRIST

You perform then, that we may see it and believe You?" they ask. "What work will You do?" They point to Moses, who gave the Israelites manna in the wilderness. Jesus tells them that it is God and not Moses who "gives you the true bread from heaven. For the bread of God is He who comes down from heaven and gives life to the world."

"Lord, give us this bread always," the people reply. Jesus then astounds them by saying: "I am the bread of life. He who comes to Me shall never hunger and he who believes in Me shall never thirst." The will of God is that anyone who sees the Son and believes in Him have everlasting life.

At this, the crowd begins to murmur against Him. They refuse to believe that this man, whose family they know, can have come from heaven. "Is not this Jesus, the son of Joseph, whose father and mother we know?" they complain. "Do not murmur among yourselves," Jesus says. "No one can come to me unless the Father who sent me draws him."

"Most assuredly, I say to you, he who believes in Me has everlasting life," He says. "Your fathers ate the manna in the wilderness and are dead . . . I am the living bread which came down from heaven. If anyone eats of this bread, he will live forever." The "bread that I shall give is My flesh, which I shall give for the life of this world."

"How can this Man give us His flesh to eat?" the people wonder, quarreling among themselves. "My flesh is food indeed and My blood is drink indeed," Jesus replies. "Whoever eats My flesh and drinks My blood has eternal life, and I will raise him up on the last day."

Many of Jesus' followers are scandalized and appalled by this teaching. "This is a hard saying," they fret. "Who can understand it?" "Does this offend you?" Jesus says. "What then if you should see the Son of Man ascend where He was before? It is the Spirit who gives life; the flesh profits nothing. The words that I speak to you are spirit, and they are life."

At this point many turn away "and walked with Him no more." "Do you also want to go away?" Jesus says to the Twelve. "Lord, to whom shall we go?" Peter answers, "You have the words of eternal life." Jesus then predicts that although He chose the Twelve Himself, "one of you is a devil." By this He indicates Judas Iscariot, who will eventually betray Him.

Instruction Concerning Defilement

◄ Matthew 15:1-20
◄ Mark 7:1-23
◄ John 7:1

In Capernaum again, Pharisees and scribes from Jerusalem ask Jesus why His disciples "transgress the traditions of the elders?" They are referring here to ritual purifications before eating which Jesus' disciples do not observe. "Why do you also transgress the commandment of God?" Jesus retorts. He points out that they do many things in honor of their own traditions that repudiate God's laws.

Calling the multitude, Jesus announces that "there is nothing that enters a man from outside which can defile him." It is rather "what comes out of the heart of man" that defiles him: "Evil thoughts, adulteries, fornications, murders, thefts, covetousness, wickedness, deceit, lewdness, an evil eye, blasphemy, pride, foolishness . . . To eat with unwashed hands does not defile a man." When Jesus' disciples alert Him that the Pharisees have taken offense at His words, Jesus instructs them to "let them alone." "They are blind leaders of the blind," Jesus says, "And if the blind leads the blind both will fall into a ditch."

35 CAPERNAUM TO TYRE AND SIDON

Matthew 15:21-28 ▶
Mark 7:24-30 ▶

Healing of the Syro-Phoenecian's Daughter

Because of the religious conflicts, Jesus leaves with His disciples and travels into the region of Tyre and Sidon beyond Israel, a journey of between 40 and 50 miles heading northwest along the Mediterranean seaboard. A Greek woman here approaches Him, begging Him to cast a demon from her daughter. "Have mercy on me, O Lord, Son of David! My daughter is severely demon-possessed." Jesus tells the woman that He has not come to minister to Gentiles. "It is not good to take the children's bread and throw it to the little dogs," He explains. "Yes, Lord," the woman responds, "yet even the little dogs eat the crumbs which fall from their master's table." "O woman, great is your faith!" Jesus replies, moved by her response. "For this saying go your way; the demon has gone out of your daughter." The woman returns home to find her daughter exorcised and lying in her bed.

36 TYRE AND SIDON TO THE SEA OF GALILEE VIA THE DECAPOLIS

Matthew 15:29-38 ▶
Mark 7:31–8:9 ▶

Feeding of the Four Thousand

Departing the region of Tyre and Sidon and nearing the Sea of Galilee, Jesus meets large crowds of people. They have with them the "lame, blind, mute, and maimed." These are laid at His feet. He heals each of them, and when the multitudes see "the mute speaking, the maimed made whole, the lame walking and the blind seeing" they glorify God.

Mark details the incident of a deaf man with a speech impediment. Jesus takes the man apart from the crowd, puts His fingers in the man's ears, spits, touches His tongue, then sighs as He looks up to heaven, saying, "Ephphatha," which means "be opened." The man's ears are opened and he begins to speak without impediment. Although Jesus charges the people not to announce the miracles, the report of His works is broadcast far and wide.

He soon decides to feed the people and, calling His disciples to Him, tells them of His "compassion on the multitude." "They have now continued with Me three days," He says. "Some of them have come from afar [and] I do not want to send them away hungry lest they faint on the way."

"Where could we get enough bread in the wilderness to fill such a great multitude?" His disciples wonder. "How many loaves do you have?" Jesus says. The disciples produce seven loaves of bread and "a few little fish." Jesus gives thanks for the food and hands it to His disciples to distribute to the four thousand men and their families. The disciples collect seven baskets of food left over after everyone has eaten his fill.

37 THE SEA OF GALILEE TO MAGDALA (DALMANUTHA)

Rejection in Magdala

After Jesus dismisses the crowds, He departs for Magdala, or Dalmanutha, with His disciples. He is immediately confronted there by the Pharisees and Sadducees, who demand from Him "a sign from heaven" proving His authority. Mark writes that on hearing this request Jesus "sighed deeply in His spirit." He wonders aloud at the lack of spiritual discernment among the religious leaders. While they are well able to tell the day's weather by "the face of the sky," they are incapable of discerning "the signs of the times." "Hypocrites!" Jesus says to them, "No sign shall be given" except "the sign of the prophet Jonah."

◀ Matthew 15:39–16:4
◀ Mark 8:10-12

38 MAGDALA TO BETHSAIDA

Warning Against the Leaven of the Pharisees

Jesus and His disciples depart by boat to the other side of the Sea of Galilee, but they forget to take bread for the journey, having just one loaf between them in the boat. Jesus warns His disciples to beware of "the leaven of the Pharisees and Sadducees," intending by this figure of speech to give warning against their doctrines. The disciples mistake Jesus' remark as a reference to their having forgotten provisions for the trip. He upbraids them then for their slow-witted and faithless reasoning. "Do you not yet perceive nor understand? Is your heart still hardened? Having eyes, do you not see? And having ears, do you not hear? And do you not remember?"

◀ Matthew 16:5-12
◀ Mark 8:13-26

The muddled disciples must be reminded by Jesus of the miraculous events they have only just witnessed, and helped to draw what should be obvious conclusions: "When I broke the five loaves for the five thousand, how many baskets of fragments did you take up?" Jesus demands. "Twelve," they say. "When I broke the seven for the four thousand, how many large baskets full of fragments did you take up?" "Seven," they say. "How is it you do not understand?" Jesus wonders, dismayed by their incomprehension.

When they arrive at Bethsaida, a blind man is brought to Jesus by the people who "begged Him to touch him." Jesus takes the man by the hand and leads him out of the village. He spits on the man's eyes, lays His hands on him, and asks him whether he sees anything. "I see men like trees, walking," the man answers. Jesus lays His hands on him again and the man's sight is fully restored.

39 BETHSAIDA TO CAESAREA PHILIPPI

Peter's Confession

Matthew 16:13-20 ▶
Mark 8:27-30 ▶
Luke 9:18-21 ▶

"Who do men say that I, the Son of Man, am?" Jesus asks His disciples in Caesarea Philipi. "Some say John the Baptist," they reply, "some Elijah, and others Jeremiah or one of the prophets." "But who do you say that I am?" Jesus asks. "You are the Christ, the Son of the living God," Peter responds. Jesus praises him for his confession of faith: "Blessed are you Simon Bar-Jonah, for flesh and blood has not revealed this to you, but my Father who is in heaven." "You are Peter," Jesus says, and "on this rock I will build My church." His disciples are then charged not to tell anyone that He is "Jesus, the Christ."

First Prediction of Death and Peter's Rebuke

Matthew 16:21-26 ▶
Mark 8:31-37 ▶
Luke 9:22-25 ▶

Jesus begins telling His disciples explicitly of the imminent persecution and death He will face in Jerusalem. There the religious leaders will reject Him. He will suffer "many things from the elders and chief priests and scribes and be killed" but rise again on the third day. At this Peter takes Jesus aside and reproaches Him, "Far be it from You Lord; this shall not happen to You."

Having just praised Peter for his divinely inspired confession, Jesus now repudiates his counsel as prompted by the devil. "Get thee behind Me, Satan!" He says to Peter, "You are an offense to Me." He then turns to His disciples and insists that if anyone desires to follow Him, he must be prepared to give up his life. "What," Jesus asks, "will a man give in exchange for his soul?" And "what will it profit a man if he gains the whole world" at the cost of his soul? Jesus' call offers no middle ground: to be His disciple is to face death. Anyone who aims to serve himself and Christ will necessarily forfeit both.

First Prediction of His Second Coming

Jesus warns that "whoever is ashamed of Me and My words in this adulterous and sinful generation, of him the Son of Man also will be ashamed when He comes in the glory of His Father with the holy angels." He promises them that some of His listeners "will not taste death" before they see the kingdom of God come in power and glory. This advent is begun with Jesus' death and resurrection, but awaits its culmination at the hour of His return.

◄ Matthew 16:27-28
◄ Mark 8:38–9:1
◄ Luke 9:26-27

Conclusion

There are many things the disciples should have learned from the encounters covered in this chapter. Witnessing Jesus and one of their own literally walking on water might have convinced them of Jesus' divine potency. His feeding of the crowds is a demonstration of His care for the physical as well as the spiritual needs of people and not merely a raw exercise of supernatural power.

The disciples are further introduced to the difficult nature of Jesus' teachings, which have here become a scandal and a stumbling block for many. They see that His uncompromising message is without special accommodation to the religious leadership. Nor do they as His friends escape its call to self-sacrifice. Jesus teaches His disciples that, while God's kingdom is misunderstood and rejected by many, it is nevertheless open to all those who believe.

The Training of the Twelve and Others

Jesus continues to devote time to training the Twelve. He is imparting to them the principles that must govern the lives of believers after His earthly ministry ends. They will soon bear responsibility for disseminating the good news of His kingdom to the world. Note again in this chapter how Jesus uses each encounter to instruct them.

Spring/Summer A.D. 29

40 CAESAREA PHILIPPI TO MOUNT HERMON

The Transfiguration

Six days later Jesus leads Peter, James, and John north onto Mount Hermon. Here He is transfigured before them. His face "shone like the sun" and His clothes glisten, becoming "as white as light" or snow "such as no launderer on earth can whiten them." With Him appear Elijah and Moses. They are discussing His impending death in Jerusalem when Peter blurts out: "Lord, it is good for us to be here. If You wish, let us make here three tabernacles: one for You, one for Moses, and one for Elijah." At this a bright cloud overshadows Peter, James, and John and a voice from the cloud utters the words, **"This is My beloved Son. Hear Him!"** The three disciples fall on their faces in fear. Jesus touches them. "Arise, and do not be afraid," He says. When they look up, Jesus is alone.

◄ Matthew 17:1-8
◄ Mark 9:2-8
◄ Luke 9:28-36

Jesus Identifies John with Elijah

On the way down the mountain, Jesus urges the three to "tell the vision to no one until the Son of Man is risen from the dead." The disciples wonder among themselves what Jesus means by "risen from the dead," and ask Him why "the scribes say Elijah must come first." They are referring here to the belief that the coming of an "Elijah" must predate the coming of the Messiah. Jesus answers that Elijah must indeed come first as the prophet Malachi foretold (see Malachi 4:5-6), but that Elijah in the person of John the Baptist has come already. He was mistreated and rejected. "They did not know him but did to him whatever they wished," Jesus says. In the same way the Son of Man will also "suffer at their hands."

◄ Matthew 17:9-13
◄ Mark 9:9-13
◄ Luke 9:36

The Disciples' Failed Exorcism

When Jesus and the three rejoin the others, they find a large crowd gathered and His disciples disputing with some scribes. The crowd sees Jesus and runs to greet Him. "What are you discussing with

◄ Matthew 17:14-21
◄ Mark 9:14-29
◄ Luke 9:37-42

them?" Jesus asks. "Teacher, I brought to You my son, who has a mute spirit," a man answers. Whenever the spirit seizes the boy it "throws him down; he foams at the mouth, gnashes his teeth and becomes rigid. So I spoke to Your disciples that they should cast it out but they could not." "O faithless and perverse generation," Jesus says, "how long shall I be with you? Bring him to me."

In Jesus' presence the spirit convulses the boy and "he fell on the ground and wallowed, foaming at the mouth." "How long has this been happening to him?" Jesus asks the boy's father. "From childhood. And often he has thrown him both into the fire and into the water to destroy him. But if You can do anything, have compassion on us and help us." "If you can believe, all things are possible to him who believes," Jesus replies. "Lord, I believe; help my unbelief!" the man answers.

At this point Jesus rebukes the unclean spirit: "Deaf and dumb spirit, I command you, come out of him and enter him no more." The spirit departs with a cry, convulsing the boy once more. Afterward he lies motionless. "He is dead," the crowd thinks. But Jesus takes the boy by his hand, lifts him up and presents him to his father exorcised and healed. Privately the disciples ask Jesus why they were unable to cast the demon out. "Because of your unbelief," Jesus tells them, but adds that this kind of demon "does not go out except by prayer and fasting."

41 MOUNT HERMON TO GALILEE

Prediction of His Resurrection

Matthew 17:22-23 ▶
Mark 9:30-32 ▶
Luke 9:43-45 ▶

Jesus and the disciples depart from Mount Hermon and discreetly pass through Galilee. Jesus does not want anyone to know they have arrived since He hopes to avoid the distractions of His public ministry. "Let these words sink down into your ears," Jesus tells His disciples. "The Son of Man is about to be betrayed into the hands of men . . . and after He is killed, He will rise on the third day." The disciples still do not understand what He means but they are sorry to hear these grim pronouncements and afraid to question Him further.

42 GALILEE TO CAPERNAUM

Jesus Pays the Temple Tax

Matthew 17:24-27 ▶

When the group arrives in Capernaum, the Temple tax collectors ask Peter whether Jesus pays the half-shekel Temple tax prescribed in the Torah (see Exodus 30:11-15). Peter answers yes. Later, Jesus broaches the subject with him. "What do you think, Simon? From whom do the kings of the earth take customs or taxes, from their sons or from strangers?" "From strangers," Peter answers. In that case, Jesus reasons, "the sons are free." By this analogy He implies that as the Son of God, He is exempt from the Temple tax. "Nevertheless, lest we offend them, go to the sea, cast a hook, and take the fish that comes up first." In its mouth Peter will find a shekel to cover the tax for both of them.

Competition Among the Twelve

In Capernaum, the disciples fall to disputing among themselves about who is to be "greatest in the kingdom of heaven." Jesus tells them that "if anyone desires to be first, he shall be last of all and servant of all." To illustrate His point, Jesus takes a little child into His arms and instructs His disciples that unless they become themselves like little children, they will not enter the kingdom of heaven. He teaches them that "whoever receives one of these little children in My name receives Me," and that whoever "receives Me" receives "Him who sent Me."

◄ Matthew 18:1-5
◄ Mark 9:33-37
◄ Luke 9:46-48

Instruction Concerning Offenses

While still in Capernaum, John informs Jesus that the disciples have found someone casting out demons in His name without their permission. "We forbade him because he does not follow us," John tells Jesus. "Do not forbid him," Jesus replies. "No one who works a miracle in My name can soon afterward speak evil of Me. For he who is not against us is on our side." He promises that God will reward anyone who aids them "because you belong to Christ," but warns that divine punishment awaits anyone causing "one of these little ones who believe in Me to stumble." Jesus advises the disciples that "it would be better [for such a person] if a millstone were hung around his neck, and he were drowned in the depth of the sea."

◄ Matthew 18:6-14
◄ Mark 9:38-50
◄ Luke 9:49-50

"Woe to the world because of offenses!" Jesus tells them. For while "offenses must come . . . woe to that man by whom the offense comes!" If your hand or foot causes you to sin "cut it off," and if it is your eye that misguides you "pluck it out and cast it from you," since "it is better for you to enter life maimed" than to be cast into hell in one piece. "Their worm does not die," Jesus says of the damned, and hell fire "shall never be quenched."

Like a man who has a hundred sheep with just one gone astray, God seeks the one who is lost and rejoices when that one returns to Him. It is God's desire that no one stumble or fall away.

Instruction Concerning Forgiveness

Jesus teaches His disciples that when you are wronged, you should go first to the offending person in private and "tell him his fault." If he refuses to listen, find "one or two more" to approach him with you that "by the mouth of two or three witnesses every word may be established." In the case of continued stubborn resistance, the church should address the matter. If the person remains defiant, repelling all attempts at peace, the church must then treat him as if he were "a heathen and a tax collector." Of course, Jesus' command is that we love and minister to believers and unbelievers alike, but here Jesus gives the church instruction and authority to deal with unrepented sin among believers.

◄ Matthew 18:15-35

"Lord, how often shall my brother sin against me, and I forgive him? Up to seven times?" Not seven, "but up to seventy times seven," Jesus answers. He illustrates with the parable of a servant indebted to his master in the sum of "ten thousand talents." Since he is quite unable to pay when the time comes to settle accounts, the master orders that "he be sold, with his wife and children and all that he had." The man beseeches his master to have patience with him and renews his promise to pay him in full. The master, "moved with compassion," simply cancels the debt.

That servant then meets a fellow servant who owes him a comparatively very small sum, a mere hundred denarii. He seizes the man by his throat and demands, "Pay me what you owe!" His fellow servant falls down at his feet pleading with him to have patience. "I will pay you all," he promises him. Unmoved by this appeal, the man forgiven much has his debtor thrown into prison till he should pay his debt. The other servants witnessing this behavior are "very grieved" and report the matter to their master, who punishes the unforgiving servant for his lack of mercy. "Should you not also have had compassion on your fellow servant, just as I had pity on you?" the master demands. By this analogy Jesus argues that "each of you," whom God has forgiven much, must also "from his heart" forgive "his brother his trespasses."

Cost of Discipleship

Matthew 8:19-22 ▶
Luke 9:57-62 ▶

At this point a "certain scribe" approaches Jesus vowing, "Teacher, I will go with You wherever You go." "Foxes have holes and birds of the air have nests," Jesus says, "but the Son of Man has nowhere to lay His head." Another requests permission to "first go bury my father." "Let the dead bury their own dead," Jesus tells him. Still another asks leave to bid farewell to those "who are at my house." "No one, having put his hand to the plow, and looking back is fit for the kingdom of God," Jesus replies. The sense of Jesus' words is that the cost of discipleship is steep and may include the surrender of all that is held most dear.

Challenge From Jesus' Brothers

John 7:2-9 ▶

The Feast of Tabernacles, or Sukkoth, is now at hand, and Jesus' brothers challenge Him to go to Jerusalem and declare Himself if He is indeed the Messiah. "No one does anything in secret while he himself seeks to be known openly," they advise Him. "If You do these things, show Yourself to the world." There is a note of derision in this challenge since His brothers do not believe He is the Messiah. "Your time is always ready," Jesus tells them, "my time has not yet come." He points out that the world does not hate them as it hates Him. "It hates Me because I testify that its works are evil." So "you go up to this feast," Jesus tells them, "My time has not yet fully come."

43 FROM CAPERNAUM TO SAMARIA

The Journey to Jerusalem

◀ Luke 9:51-56
◀ John 7:10

Not long afterward, Jesus sets off privately for Jerusalem with His disciples. On the way, they come to a Samaritan village that shuns Him. The Samaritans do not worship at Jerusalem, and so want nothing to do with this group travelling there for the feast. James and John are carried away by spite: "Lord, do You want us to command fire to come down from heaven and consume them just as Elijah did?" "The Son of Man did not come to destroy men's lives," Jesus tells the hot-tempered disciples, "but to save them."

Conclusion

This chapter has included no major encounters with the religious leadership. Jesus has used this time to focus on the Twelve. The most significant event here is the Transfiguration, a further confirmation of Jesus' identity as the Son of God. Peter refers to this event in his own writings as an undeniable demonstration of Jesus' divine nature (see 2 Peter 1:16-21). Jesus continues to use encounters in their lives together to teach the disciples lessons on humility, forgiveness, faith, and discipleship.

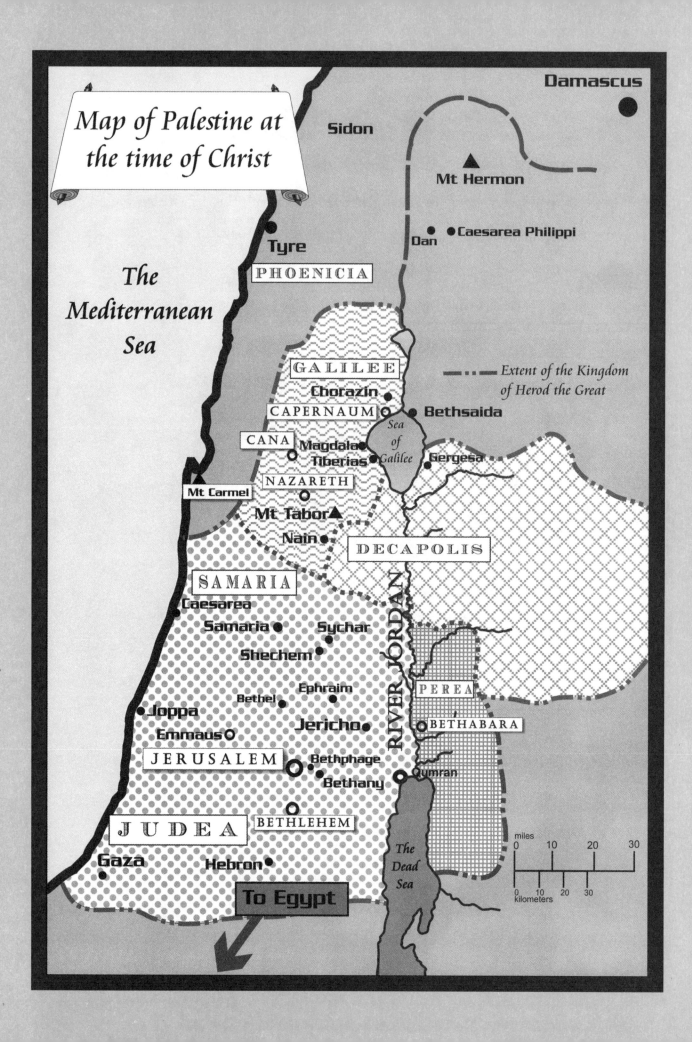

The Later Judean Ministry

Jesus returns to Jerusalem to face renewed attacks by the religious leaders. In the days to come, the disciples will become targets of hostility as they work to establish the New Covenant church. The disciples learn from Jesus how to deal with opposition from authorities.

Fall, A.D. 29

44   SAMARIA TO JERUSALEM

Conflicts with the Priests in Jerusalem

◄ John 7:11-52

"Where is He?" the people wonder during the Feast of Tabernacles in Jerusalem. John writes that there is "much complaining among the people concerning Him." Some say, "He is good," while others claim, "No. On the contrary, He deceives the people." No one dares discuss Him publicly, though, for fear of persecution by the religious leaders. About halfway through the weeklong feast, Jesus appears in the Temple teaching.

Here the people marvel at His wisdom: "How does this Man know letters, having never studied?" they wonder. "My teaching is not Mine but His who sent Me," Jesus answers. "If anyone wills to do His will, he shall know concerning the doctrine, whether it is from God or whether I speak on My own authority." A readiness to obey is the precondition for spiritual discernment.

"Did not Moses give you the law, yet none of you keeps the law?" Jesus asks them. Why then "do you seek to kill me?" "You have a demon. Who is seeking to kill You?" the people retort. Others recognize that Jesus is indeed the man the religious leaders are plotting to kill: "But look! He speaks boldly and they say nothing to Him. Do the rulers know indeed that this is truly the Christ?" Still others argue that Jesus cannot be the Christ since they know where He is from. They are appealing here to a widely held belief that the Christ must remain hidden until the day of His coming.

"You both know Me, and you know where I am from," Jesus announces. "I know Him, for I am from Him, and He sent Me." By this He indicates His divine origin and destiny, infuriating the religious leaders. These move to arrest Him for blasphemy and yet no one lays a hand on Him "because His hour had not yet come." Many of the people believe Jesus because they cannot imagine anyone performing greater corroborating signs and wonders: "When the Christ comes, will He give more signs than this man has?"

The religious leaders overhear people reasoning in this vein, and dispatch officers to arrest Him. Jesus tells the people that He will be with them only a little while longer. He must soon return to God.

The people do not understand. They think Jesus is planning to join other Jews living in the Diaspora (the *dispersion*, or *scattering* of the Jews from Israel due to war, captivity, and persecution) beyond Israel's borders. "Is He intending to go abroad to the people who are dispersed among the Greeks and to teach the Greeks?"

On the last day of the feast, Jesus stands and cries out, "If anyone thirsts, let Him come to Me and drink. He who believes in Me, as the Scripture has said, out of his heart will flow rivers of living water." The image is a reference to the Holy Spirit, whom He will send to believers after His resurrection and ascension to heaven. On the strength of this saying many in the crowd conclude that "truly, this is the Prophet." Many others decide, "This is the Christ." Adding to the confusion is their knowledge from Scripture that "the Christ comes from the seed of David and from the town of Bethlehem," while the prevailing assumption is that Jesus is from Nazareth in Galilee.

The officers sent by the religious leaders to arrest Jesus return empty-handed. "Why have you not brought Him?" the leaders demand. "No man ever spoke like this man," the officers reply. "Are you also deceived?" the Pharisees scoff. "Have any of the rulers or the Pharisees believed in Him?" As for "this crowd that does not know the law," it is both ignorant and "accursed." Nicodemus, who is one of the leaders but also privately a believer, urges tolerance. "Does our law judge a man before it hears him and knows what he is doing?" he asks. "Are you also from Galilee?" the Pharisees deride him, "Search and look, for no prophet has arisen out of Galilee."

John 7:53–8:11 ▶

The Woman Caught in Adultery

Everyone returns home except Jesus, who goes up to the Mount of Olives. The next morning He returns to the Temple to teach. The scribes and Pharisees bring to Him a woman caught in adultery, and ask for His judgment since the Mosaic Law indicates that adulterers should be stoned. The Pharisees mean in this to set a trap for Him.

If He answers that the woman should not be stoned, He flouts the Law of Moses. If He decides in favor of stoning her, He violates the Roman laws against murder. Ignoring the question Jesus stoops down and begins writing in the sand with His finger. He then brilliantly turns the tables on their ploy. "He who is without sin among you," Jesus says to them, "let him throw a stone at her first."

The woman's accusers are silenced and, conscience-ridden, file away beginning with the eldest among them. Jesus soon finds Himself alone with the woman. "Woman, where are those accusers of yours?" He asks. "Has no one condemned you?" "No one, Lord," she answers. "Neither do I condemn you," He says, "Go and sin no more."

Light of the World

◄ John 8:12-20

"I am the light of the world," Jesus announces, standing in the treasury of the Temple, "He who follows me shall not walk in darkness, but have the light of life." The Pharisees with Him dispute that "You bear witness of Yourself. Your witness is not true." Jesus assures them that His testimony is true, and that His Father testifies in its behalf, thereby fulfilling the legal requirement that two witnesses substantiate a claim. "Where is Your Father?" the Pharisees demand. "You know neither Me nor My Father," Jesus says. Their rejection of Him is proof of this.

Jesus Confronts the Crowd

◄ John 8:21-59

"I am going away, and you will seek Me, and will die in your sins. Where I am going you cannot come," Jesus says to them. Does this mean "He will kill Himself?" the Jews wonder. "You are from beneath; I am from above. You are of this world; I am not of this world," Jesus continues. "If you do not believe that I am He, you will die in your sins." "Who are You?" the people reply. "Just what I have been saying to you from the beginning . . . He who sent Me is true; and I speak to the world those things which I heard from Him," Jesus says.

"And He who sent Me is with Me. The Father has not left Me alone, for I always do those things that please Him." Many of His listeners accept this testimony. Jesus tells them that they can prove the worth of their dicipleship by their obedience to His word. They will know truth that will make them free. At this, the would-be disciples protest, "We are Abraham's descendants, and have never been in bondage to anyone. How can you say 'You will be made free?'" "Whoever commits sin is a slave to sin," Jesus replies. "And a slave does not abide in the house forever." Only a son abides forever. "Therefore if the Son makes you free, you shall be free indeed."

"Abraham is our father," the people proclaim. "If you were Abraham's children, you would do the works of Abraham," Jesus tells them. "We were not born of fornication," the Jews fire back. This is perhaps an especially barbed attack on the strange circumstances of Jesus' birth, implying that He is the product of an illicit and carnal union. "We have one Father—God."

"If God were your father you would love Me, for I proceeded forth and came from God," Jesus retorts. "You are of your father the devil! . . . He was a murderer from the beginning [and when he speaks] he is a liar and the father of it . . . But because I tell the truth, you do not believe me."

"Which of you convicts Me of sin?" Jesus challenges. His claim to be the Son of God would be forever discredited if He were so convicted but He is certain of His person and the truth of His words: "He who is of God hears God's words; therefore you do not hear, because you are not of God."

The people are of course offended by this denunciation. "Do we not say rightly that You are a Samaritan and have a demon?" they jeer. "I honor My Father and you dishonor Me," Jesus says. "Most assuredly I say to you, if anyone keeps My word he shall never see death."

"Now we know that You have a demon! Abraham is dead, and the prophets; and You say, 'If anyone keeps my word he shall never taste death.'" The affront and presumption of this statement is unbearable. "Who do you make yourself out to be?" they demand. "Are you greater than our father Abraham, who is dead?"

"If I honor Myself, My honor is nothing," Jesus says. "It is My Father who honors Me." He tells them that Abraham himself looked forward with the eyes of faith to the advent of His coming. "Your father Abraham rejoiced to see My day, and he saw it and was glad."

"You are not yet fifty years old," the people scoff, "and have You seen Abraham?" "Most assuredly, I say to you," Jesus answers, "before Abraham was, I AM." Incensed, the crowd takes up stones to kill Him for claiming to be God but Jesus hides himself and departs the Temple, passing through the midst of them unharmed.

John 9:1-41 ▶

Healing of the Man Born Blind

Soon afterward Jesus encounters a man on the Sabbath "who was blind from birth." "Rabbi, who sinned, this man or his parents, that he was born blind?" His disciples inquire. "Neither this man nor his parents," Jesus replies. Rather it was so "that the works of God should be revealed in him . . . As long as I am in the world, I am the light of the world," Jesus says. He then spits on the ground and makes clay with the saliva, anointing the eyes of the blind man with the clay and ordering him to wash in the pool of Siloam. The man washes his eyes in the pool and returns seeing.

Eventually he is taken to the Pharisees by his neighbors who wonder, "Is this not he who sat and begged?" Others are not so sure, noting a distinct resemblance to the blind beggar. "He is like him," they say. "I am he," the man born blind tells them. Then "how were your eyes opened?" they ask. The man recounts the events of his healing for them as well as for the Pharisees who fall to disputing among themselves. "This Man is not from God, because he does not keep the Sabbath," some say. "How can a man who is a sinner do such signs?" others wonder.

"What do you say about Him because He opened your eyes?"they demand of the beggar. "He is a prophet," the man replies. The Pharisees send for the man's parents for confirmation that he is indeed the same man who was born blind. "We know that this is our son, and that he was born blind," the man's parents tell them. "How then does he now see?" they demand. "We do not know," his parents reply, hoping to avoid a conflict with the Jews which might get them barred from the synagogue. "He is of age; ask him. He will speak for himself."

The Pharisees resummon the man. "Give God the glory! We know that this Man is a sinner," they tell him. "Whether He is a sinner or not I do not know," the man replies. "One thing I know: that though I was blind, now I see."The Pharisees ask him to recount the miracle. "What did He do to you? How did he open your eyes?" "Why do you want to hear it again?" the man says. "I told you already and you did not listen . . . Do you also want to become His disciples?" "You are His disciple," the Pharisees revile him, "but we are Moses' disciples. We know that God spoke to Moses; as for this fellow, we do not know where He is from." "Why, this is a marvelous thing," the man replies, "that you do not know where He is from . . . Since the world began it has been unheard of that anyone opened the eyes of one who was born blind. If this man were not from God He could do nothing." "You were completely born in sins," the Pharisees sneer, "and you are teaching us?" Finally they cast the man from the synagogue.

Hearing that the man was cast out, Jesus searches for him and finds him. "Do you believe in the Son of God?" Jesus asks him. "Who is He, Lord, that I may believe in Him?" the man replies. "You have both seen Him and it is He Who is talking with you," Jesus says. "Lord, I believe!" the man confesses.

It is "for judgment that I have come into this world, that those who do not see may see and that those who see may be made blind," Jesus explains. When some Pharisees with Jesus ask if "we are blind also," Jesus tells them that if they were blind they would be guiltless. "But now you say, 'We see,' therefore your sin remains."

The Good Shepherd

◄ John 10:1-21

Using the imagery of sheep, a shepherd, and the gate of a sheepfold, Jesus teaches His listeners that He is the one true way to God. He calls Himself the good shepherd, who cares for His sheep and lays down His life to protect them from their enemies. He mentions other sheep "not of this fold" that He will gather, referring to the Gentiles who will later make one flock with the Jews. Of His death for sin, Jesus explains that He lays down His life of His own accord and that God has granted Him the power to take it up again. Again the crowd is divided because of His teaching. "He has a demon and is mad," some say, "why do you listen to Him?" "Can a demon open the eyes of the blind?" others pointedly inquire.

45 JERUSALEM TO THE VILLAGES OF JUDEA

Luke 10:1-24 ▶

The Mission of the Seventy

Now Jesus selects 70 other disciples and sends them out in pairs to the cities where He will teach. He tells them that "the harvest is truly great, but the laborers are few." They will be as "lambs among wolves," carrying neither money nor extra clothes, and are not to get distracted along the way. They should rely on the hospitality of people in each town they visit. If rejected they must keep going. Jesus warns of the judgment awaiting those who resist His disciples: "He who hears you hears Me, he who rejects you rejects Me, and he who rejects Me rejects Him who sent me." These disciples must go into the cities to preach the kingdom of God and to heal the sick.

The disciples return from their mission rejoicing: "Lord, even the demons are subject to us in Your name." "I saw Satan fall like lightning from heaven," Jesus tells them. He warns them, however, against exulting in their authority over demons, and urges them to be glad instead that their names are written in heaven.

Jesus then says a prayer of thanksgiving to His Father for using these simple people: "I thank You, Father, Lord of heaven and earth, that You have hidden these things from the wise and prudent and revealed them to babes." He proclaims His disciples blessed for the privilege of witnessing themselves the coming of the kingdom of God, something many prophets and kings before them longed to see but did not.

Luke 10:25-37 ▶

The Good Samaritan

Later a lawyer puts Jesus to the test by asking Him, "What shall I do to inherit eternal life?" Jesus asks him what he thinks he should do, and the lawyer answers according to his knowledge of the Law that a man should love God with all his heart, soul, strength, and mind, and love his neighbor as himself. Jesus agrees. "Do this and you will live," He tells the lawyer.

But the lawyer, "wanting to justify himself," asks, "And who is my neighbor?" In reply, Jesus tells the parable of the Good Samaritan. The story is that of a man who journeying from Jerusalem to Jericho is waylaid by thieves. They leave him robbed, beaten, naked, and half dead by the side of the road. A priest passes by and refuses to help him, likewise a Levite. Perhaps they think the man dead and fear they will be made ritually unclean by touching him. Maybe they are themselves afraid of being attacked and so hurry on their way.

Eventually a Samaritan, an enemy of the Jews, passes by. He has compassion on the man, bandages his wounds, "pouring on oil and wine," and, after setting him on his own animal, conducts him to an inn where he cares for him. The next morning he pays the innkeeper to take care of him, promising to repay "whatever more you spend when I come again." "So which of these three do you think was neighbor to him who fell among thieves?" Jesus asks the lawyer. "He who showed mercy on him," the lawyer answers. "Go and do likewise," Jesus says.

46 JUDEA TO BETHANY AND THE VILLAGES OF JUDEA

Jesus with Mary and Martha

◄ Luke 10:38-42

Jesus then enters Bethany where a woman named Martha welcomes Him into her house. There Martha's sister Mary sits at Jesus' feet and listens to Him teach, while Martha is busy serving her guests. "Lord do You not care that my sister has left me to serve alone?" Martha complains. "Therefore tell her to help me." "Martha, Martha," Jesus corrects her, "you are worried and troubled about many things. But one thing is needed, and Mary has chosen that good part, which will not be taken away from her."

The Lord's Prayer

◄ Luke 11:1-13

After concluding His prayers one day, Jesus is asked by His disciples to teach them how to pray, "as John [the Baptist] also taught his disciples." Jesus gives them the Lord's Prayer as a model to use for their own prayers. It teaches that prayer should include:

- Adoration and praise for God

- Seeking God's will

- Asking for our daily needs

- Confession of sins

- Forgiveness of others

- Asking for strength to endure temptation

- Asking for protection from evil

Jesus compares God to a man whose friend comes by late at night with a request for bread. Though it is late, the man will give his friend what he asks if only to get rid of him. Arguing in a similar fashion, Jesus inquires whether a son asking his father for an egg should expect to receive from him a scorpion? Or when he asks for bread, is he given a stone? Jesus reasons that even sinful humans know how to give good gifts to their children. "How much more" then does their heavenly Father "give the Holy Spirit" to those who ask.

The Sign of Jonah
Luke 11:14-36 ▶

When Jesus casts a demon from a mute, some in the crowd, echoing the views of the Pharisees, claim He does so by the power of Beelzebub, the ruler of the demons, while others challenge Him to produce a sign from heaven compelling them to believe. "If Satan also is divided against himself, how will his kingdom stand?" Jesus asks them. "And if I cast out demons by Beelzebub, by whom do your sons cast them out?" As He speaks, a woman in the crowd cries out: "Blessed is the womb that bore You, and the breasts which nursed You!" "More than that, blessed are those who hear the word of God and keep it," Jesus retorts.

To those seeking a sign, Jesus warns again that they will receive no sign except that given in Scripture. As Jonah became a sign to the city of Nineveh, calling it to repent, "so also the Son of Man will be to this generation."

Condemnation of the Pharisees and Lawyers
Luke 11:37-54 ▶

An unsuspecting Pharisee invites Jesus to dinner and is surprised when He does not perform the ritual cleansing. Jesus reproves him and his fellow Pharisees for emphasizing outward displays of obedience at the expense of more important commandments like love and justice. "Now you Pharisees make the outside of the cup and dish clean," He says to them, "but your inward part is full of greed and wickedness. Foolish ones! Did not He who made the outside make the inside also?"

Jesus then issues a series of stern denunciations. "But woe to you Pharisees! For you tithe mint and rue and all manner of herbs, and pass by justice and the love of God." Their arrogance is evidenced by their love of the best seats in the synagogues and greetings in the market places. "Woe to you scribes and Pharisees, hypocrites! For you are like graves which are not seen, and the men who walk over them are not aware of them."

A lawyer at the dinner complains: "Teacher, by saying these things You reproach us also." "Woe to you also, lawyers!" Jesus tells him. "For you load men with burdens hard to bear, and you yourselves do not touch the burdens with one of your fingers." In this He rebukes them for making the Law oppressive by adding to it ever more stringent and convoluted requirements instead of helping people to obey.

These teachers of the Law, whose job it is to expound the Scriptures, have themselves spurned obedience to the Scriptures. "Woe to you lawyers! For you have taken away the key of knowledge," Jesus continues. "You did not enter in yourselves, and those who were entering in you hindered." He calls them the direct descendants of those who killed the prophets, "for they indeed killed them, and you build their tombs." For their complicity "the blood of all the prophets which was shed from the foundation of the world" will be "required of this generation, from the blood of Abel to the blood of Zechariah who perished between the altar and the temple." The lawyers and Pharisees are inflamed by Jesus condemnations, and so begin to "assail him vehemently and to cross examine Him about many things, lying in wait for Him and seeking to catch Him in something He might say."

The Warning of the Rich Fool

◄ Luke 12:1-59

Later Jesus addresses Himself to the crowds. He warns them about the hypocrisy of the Pharisees, and advises them to fear God rather than human beings. "Teacher, tell my brother to divide the inheritance with me," a man in the crowd calls out. "Man, who made Me a judge or an arbiter over you?" Jesus counters. He cautions the man "to beware of covetousness" since "one's life does not consist in the abundance of the things he possesses."

He then tells them the parable of a rich fool who builds voluminous barns to hold the increase of his goods. The man is well pleased with himself and looks forward to enjoying his possessions for many years. One night God demands from him his soul. The man is a fool for being so preoccupied with himself and his possessions on earth that he stands empty-handed in the world to come.

By this parable Jesus teaches the importance of putting God's kingdom ahead of earthly kingdoms. He warns that He will return at an hour the people least expect. They must be alert and watch for His return. He promises reward to those servants He finds working when He returns, and assures reprisals against the unfaithful and ill-prepared.

Repent or Perish

◄ Luke 13:1-9

When the people relay news of certain Galileans "whose blood Pilate had mingled with their sacrifices," Jesus redirects their attention to themselves. "Do you suppose that these Galileans were worse sinners than all other Galileans because they suffered such things?" What about "those eighteen on whom the tower in Siloam fell?" Were they "worse sinners than all other men who dwelt in Jerusalem?" He advises them that unless they repent of their own sins, they will likewise perish.

Jesus likens the people to a fig tree. Its owner has waited an unavailing three years for the tree to bear fruit. In the end he approaches the keeper of his vineyard and says to him: "Look, for three years I have come seeking fruit on this fig tree and find none. Cut it down; why does it use up the ground?" But the keeper prevails on the owner to give him time to further cultivate the tree: "Sir, let it alone this year also, until I dig around it and fertilize it. And if it bears fruit, well. But if not, after that you can cut it down." In the same way, God patiently withholds judgment until He has given the people every opportunity to repent.

Luke 13:10-21 ▸

Healing of the Crippled Woman

Teaching in the synagogue on the Sabbath, Jesus is approached by a woman in the congregation who has for 18 years suffered a "spirit of infirmity." The woman is doubled over and can "in no way raise herself up." Jesus lays His hands on the woman and says to her, "Woman, you are loosed from your infirmity." The woman immediately stands up straight, glorifying God.

The ruler of the synagogue becomes angry with Jesus for healing on the Sabbath and announces: "There are six days on which men ought to work; therefore come and be healed on them, and not on the Sabbath day." "Hypocrite!" Jesus rebukes him, "Does not each one of you on the Sabbath loose his ox or donkey from the stall, and lead it away to water it?" That being the case, "ought not this woman, being a daughter of Abraham, whom Satan has bound — think of it — for eighteen years, be loosed from this bond on the Sabbath?"

47 THE JUDEAN TOUR TO JERUSALEM

John 10:22-39 ▸

Jesus at the Feast of Dedication

While walking in the Temple during Chanukah (the Feast of Dedication) the religious leaders surround Him, insisting that He tell them if He is the Messiah. "How long do You keep us in doubt?" they demand. "If You are the Christ, tell us plainly." Jesus points out that He has already told them. "The works that I do in My Father's name, they bear witness to Me," Jesus says. The reason they do not believe in Him is that they do not believe in God. "My sheep hear My voice, and I know them and they follow Me. And I give them eternal life, and they shall never perish . . .You do not believe, because you are not of My sheep."

Jesus assures them that those whom the Father has entrusted to Him can never be snatched away, because the Father "is greater than all" and "I and My Father are one." At this His interrogators pick up stones to stone Him. "Many good works I have shown you from My Father," Jesus says, "for which of those works do you stone Me?" "For a good work we do not stone You, but for blasphemy," the Jews answer, "because You, being a Man, make Yourself God."

Jesus replies from Psalm 82:6, where human judges are referred to as gods. If Scripture itself refers to men as gods, why do they find fault with Him "whom the Father sanctified and sent" for claiming to be God's Son? Even if you cannot believe Me, Jesus reasons, believe the works that I do and realize that these things cannot happen unless "the Father is in Me and I in Him." At this the men attempt to seize Jesus, but He escapes.

Conclusion

In the face of opposition from the religious leaders and crowds, Jesus continues to tell His listeners exactly who He is and why He has come. The intensity of His warnings and condemnations for His opponents is matched only by His compassion and mercy toward those harassed by sin, sickness, and the hardships of the world.

The Later Perean Ministry

As the opposition in Jerusalem grows, Jesus departs Judea travelling east into Perea. The religious leaders continue to repudiate Jesus' messianic claims together with the works authenticating them. It is now the winter of A.D. 29/ 30. In the closing months of His earthly ministry Jesus continues His instruction of the Twelve.

Winter, A.D. 29/30

48   JERUSALEM TO PEREA

Withdrawal from Jerusalem

◄ John 10:40-42

Jesus departs Jerusalem on a journey that will take Him into the Perean district. He ministers near the Jordan River, where John the Baptist first baptized. Many who come to Him here confess: "John performed no sign, but all the things that John spoke about this Man were true."

Lament over Jerusalem

◄ Luke 13:22-35

While in Perea Jesus passes through a number of cities and villages. "Lord, are there few who are saved?" someone asks. "Strive to enter by the narrow gate," Jesus answers, "for many, I say to you, will seek to enter and will not be able to." He warns that when God closes the door to the kingdom there will be left outside many saying, "We ate in your presence and You taught in our streets," and "Lord, Lord, open to us." These will be repelled and barred: "I do not know where you are from. Depart from Me, all you workers of iniquity." Peering in from without they will see the patriarchs, the prophets, and Gentiles, too, and they will be sorry.

Pharisees approach Jesus warning, "Get out and depart from here, for Herod wants to kill You." "Go tell that fox," Jesus retorts, "it cannot be that a prophet should perish outside Jerusalem." But "on the third day I shall be perfected." By this, Jesus predicts the triumph of His resurrection from the dead. He will not be thrown off course by Herod's threats. Remembering Jerusalem, where He knows He must suffer rejection and death, Jesus laments: "O Jerusalem, Jerusalem, the one who kills the prophets and stones those who are sent to her! How often I wanted to gather your children together, as a hen gathers her brood under her wing, but you were not willing." You "shall not see Me," Jesus tells them, "until the time comes when you say, 'Blessed is He who comes in the name of the Lord!'"

Parable of the Great Supper

◄ Luke 14:1-24

Once again Jesus dines with some Pharisees on the Sabbath. Among them is a man suffering from edema, or dropsy. "Is it lawful to heal on the Sabbath?" Jesus asks the assembled lawyers and Pharisees. The guests refuse to answer so Jesus heals the man and sends him on his way. "Which of you, having a donkey or an ox that has fallen into a pit, will not immediately pull him out on the Sabbath day?" Jesus asks them. This question goes likewise unanswered.

Noting how the guests invited to the meal choose the best seats at the table for themselves, Jesus instructs the assembly that when they are invited to a feast they must "go and sit down in the lowest place." The glory of being later promoted by the host is preferable to the shame of being asked to relinquish your place to one more honorable than yourself. Jesus explains to them that "whoever exalts himself will be humbled" but that "he who humbles himself will be exalted." He advises hosts to invite to their feasts the poor, the maimed, the lame, the blind. "You will be blessed because they cannot repay you," Jesus tells them. Better that you be repaid for your hospitality to them "at the resurrection of the just" than enjoy the reciprocal favors of rich neighbors in this life.

At this, one of the guests blurts out, "Blessed is he who shall eat bread in the kingdom of God." Jesus responds with a parable of warning. A man gives a great supper. When it is ready he sends his servant to the invited guests. "Come, for all things are now ready," the servant announces. "But they all with one accord began to make excuses." One claims to have bought a piece of ground. "I must go and see it," he explains, "I ask you to have me excused." Another apologizes that he must try out a newly acquired "five yoke of oxen" and so cannot attend. "I have married a wife," says yet another.

The master of the house angrily directs his servant to "go out quickly into the streets and lanes of the city" and "into the highways and hedges." The servants are to find "the poor and the maimed and the lame and the blind." Compel them to come to the feast in the place of the ungrateful guests, "that my house may be filled." "None of those men who were invited," the master vows, "shall taste my supper."

Counting the Cost

Luke 14:25-35 ▶

Large crowds follow Jesus as He continues His travels about Perea. For them He spells out what it means to be a disciple by analogies that make tangible the spiritual cost required. "Which of you, intending to build a tower, does not sit down first and count the cost, whether he has enough to finish it?" If one lays the foundation and then runs out of money to complete the edifice, all who see it will mock him. "This man began to build and was not able to finish," they will jeer.

"Or what king, going to make war against another king, does not sit down first and consider whether he is able with ten thousand to meet him who comes against him with twenty thousand?" Naturally, the weaker party negotiates for peace long before the battle with its stronger enemy is joined. "So likewise, whoever of you does not forsake all that he has cannot be my disciple," Jesus tells the crowd.

In even edgier language Jesus warns that "if anyone comes to Me and does not hate his father and mother, wife and children, brothers and sisters, yes, and his own life also, he cannot be My disciple." Anything shy of total commitment is wasted effort. Salt that has lost its flavor is not fit even "for the dunghill . . . He who has ears to hear, let him hear!"

The Prodigal Son

◀ Luke 15:1-32

As the tax collectors and other sinners of Perea gather to hear Him, the scribes and Pharisees begin reproaching Jesus for the company He keeps. "This Man receives sinners and eats with them," they carp. Jesus responds in a series of parables representing God's love for the lost and sinful. "What man among you, having a hundred sheep, if he loses one of them, does not leave the ninety-nine in the wilderness, and go after the one which is lost?" On finding the lost sheep the man rejoices, calling in his friends and neighbors to celebrate. "Likewise there will be more joy in heaven over one sinner who repents than over ninety-nine just persons who need no repentance."

"Or what woman having ten silver coins, if she loses one coin, does not light a lamp, sweep the house, and search until she finds it?" When she finds the lost coin she rejoices. There is likewise "joy in the presence of the angels of God, over one sinner who repents."

In a third parable Jesus tells the story of a man with two sons, the younger of whom asks for his share of his father's inheritance early and then squanders his money by a debauched life in a far country. During a famine, the son goes to work in a man's fields feeding swine. "He would gladly have filled his stomach with the pods the swine ate," Jesus tells them. The son comes to his senses when he reasons that even his father's servants have bread enough. "I will arise and go to my father," the young man decides, "and I will say to him, 'Father, I have sinned against heaven and before you and I am no longer worthy to be called your son. Make me like one of your hired servants.'"

Jesus tells His audience that the young man's father sees him coming from far off and having compassion upon him "ran and fell on his neck and kissed him." The young man declares to his father the words of repentance he had prepared beforehand to say. But his father only calls for the servants to "bring out the best robe and put it on him, and put a ring on his hand and sandals on his feet. And bring the fatted calf here and kill it, and let us eat and be merry."

The older brother who has remained devotedly at home with his father hears the sound of music and dancing as he approaches the house from the fields. He is indignant at the celebration of his brother's return and refuses to enter the house. When his father comes out to him pleading with him to relent, he complains: "I never transgressed your commandments at any time; and yet you never gave me a young goat, that I might make merry with my friends." It strikes him as especially unjust that "as soon as this son of yours came, who has devoured your livelihood with harlots, you kill the fatted calf for him." "All that I have is yours," the father soothes him. It is nevertheless only right that "we should make merry, [since] your brother was dead and is alive again." He "was lost and is found."

Three Parables on Stewardship

Luke 16:1-17:10 ▶

Jesus adds to this the parable of a certain rich man and his steward. When the rich man learns that his servant has been wasting his goods he summons the man and says to him, "What is this I hear about you? Give an account of your stewardship."

"What shall I do?" the steward wonders, realizing that he will soon be deprived of his stewardship. In dread of the consequences, he rather soberly assesses his options. "I cannot dig," he decides, and "I am ashamed to beg."

He then calls in his master's debtors. "How much do you owe my master?" He asks the first. "A hundred measures of oil," the man answers. "Take your bill, and sit down quickly and write fifty," the steward instructs him. To another owing a hundred measures of wheat he says, "Take your bill and write eighty." He negotiates thus in hope that he will be welcomed into their houses after being relieved of his position.

Jesus tells his listeners that when the master hears of this shrewd bargaining he commends the unjust steward for his astuteness. "The sons of this world are more shrewd in their generation than the sons of light," Jesus says. He tells them to use their money, tainted as it is, "to make friends for yourselves," that when your money fails, they "may receive you into an everlasting home."

"If you have not been faithful in the unrighteous mammon, who will commit to your trust the true riches?" Jesus asks. He insists that "no servant can serve two masters." The love of God is fundamentally incompatible with the love of money. The Pharisees, who are lovers of money, deride Him when they hear this teaching. Jesus admonishes them that what is esteemed by men is worthless in God's eyes.

He tells them the parable of Lazarus, a beggar "full of sores," laid at the gate of a rich man "clothed in purple and fine linen." There the dogs "licked his sores" while he languished in hope of being fed with "the crumbs which fell from the rich man's table."

When both men die, the angels carry Lazarus to the bosom of Abraham while the rich man is damned to "torments in Hades." From his vantage in hell the rich man can see Abraham "afar off and Lazarus in his bosom." "Father Abraham," the rich man calls, "have mercy on me and send Lazarus that he may dip his finger in water and cool my tongue; for I am tormented and in flame." "Son," Abraham answers him, "remember that in your lifetime you received good things, and likewise Lazarus evil things." Now Lazarus must be comforted. It is the rich man's turn to suffer. "Besides all this," Abraham explains, "between us and you" an impassable gulf is fixed. "I beg you therefore, father," the rich man answers, "send him to my father's house, for I have five brothers, that he may testify to them, lest they also come to this place of torment."

"They have Moses and the prophets," Abraham tells him, "let them hear them." "No, father Abraham," the rich man protests, "if one goes to them from the dead, they will repent." "If they do not hear Moses and the prophets," Abraham says, "neither will they be persuaded though one rise from the dead." Jesus' parable here foreshadows His own death and resurrection. As in the story, those who refuse to believe Moses and the prophets will likewise refuse Him, even after His resurrection from the dead.

If a brother "sins against you seven times in a day, and seven times in a day returns to you saying, 'I repent,' you shall forgive him," Jesus tells His disciples. "Increase our faith," the disciples urge Him. He replies that faith as insubstantial as a mustard seed is all that is required "to say to this mulberry tree, 'Be pulled up by the roots and be planted in the sea,' and it would obey you."

He further warns them against pride in their obedience. Does the master thank his servant "because he did the things that were commanded him?" Jesus asks. Is it not rather the servant's obligation to do as he is told? "So likewise you," Jesus instructs His disciples, "when you have done all those things which you are commanded, say, 'We are unprofitable servants. We have done what was our duty to do.'" The Apostle Paul, commenting on the stewardship of human life, writes: "For we must all appear before the judgment seat of Christ; that each one may receive the things done in the body, according to what he has done, whether good or bad" (2 Corinthians 5:10).

49 PEREA TO BETHANY

The Raising of Lazarus from the Dead

◀ John 11:1-44

Jesus' Perean ministry ends when He hears that a close friend, Lazarus of Bethany, is sick. Lazarus is the brother of Mary and her sister Martha. The Gospel writer John reminds the reader here that Mary is the woman "who anointed the Lord with fragrant oil and wiped His feet with her hair." The women send word to Jesus: "Lord, behold, he whom you love is sick." When Jesus hears this He replies that "this sickness is not unto death, but for the glory of God." At this point in his account John underscores that "Jesus loved Martha and her sister and Lazarus." He writes that, instead of departing immediately, Jesus tarries two days before rounding up the disciples for the trip back to Judea.

"Our friend Lazarus sleeps," Jesus says to His disciples, "but I go that I may wake him up." The uncomprehending disciples reply that "if he sleeps he will get well." "Lazarus is dead," Jesus tells them flatly. "And I am glad for your sakes that I was not there, that you may believe." "Let us also go, that we may die with Him," Thomas replies at this sad revelation. When Jesus finally arrives in Bethany, He finds that Lazarus has been in the tomb four days.

Martha receives news that Jesus has arrived and hastens out to meet him just outside Bethany. "Lord," she says, "if You had been here my brother would not have died. But even now, I know that whatever You ask of God, God will give You."

"Your brother will rise again," Jesus tells her. "I know that he will rise again in the resurrection at the last day," Martha replies, misunderstanding the sense of Jesus' words. "I am the resurrection," Jesus says. "He who believes in Me, though he may die, he shall live. And whoever lives and believes in me shall never die. Do you believe this?" "Yes, Lord," Martha answers, "I believe that You are the Christ, the Son of God, who is to come into the world."

Martha alerts Mary that "the Teacher has come and is calling for you." At this Mary hastens to meet Him. When she sees Jesus she falls down at His feet, weeping. "Lord, if you had been here, my brother would not have died," she says. When Jesus sees Mary and the Jews who are with her weeping for the dead man He "groan[s] in spirit and [is] troubled."

"Where have you laid him?" Jesus asks them. "Lord," they say, "come and see." At this moment Jesus is Himself overcome and begins to weep. "See how He loved him," the Jews marvel. But others among them complain, "Could not this Man, who opened the eyes of the blind, also have kept this man from dying?"

Jesus arrives at the tomb "groaning in Himself." The tomb is a cave, its entrance sealed by a stone. "Take away the stone," Jesus commands. "Lord," Martha protests, "by this time there is a stench." "Did I not say to you that if you would believe you would see the glory of God?" Jesus replies. The stone is rolled away from the entrance and Jesus lifts His eyes to heaven. "Father," He prays, "I thank You that You have heard Me. And I know that You always hear Me, but because of the people who are standing by I said this, that they may believe that You sent Me."

"Lazarus," He cries in a loud voice, "come forth!" At this Lazarus emerges from the tomb "bound hand and foot with graveclothes, his face wrapped in cloth." "Loose him," Jesus commands them, "and let him go."

50   BETHANY TO EPHRAIM

Plotting Jesus' Death

◀ John 11:45-54

When news of this miracle reaches the Pharisees, a council is convened to determine a course of action. "What shall we do?" the Pharisees fret. "For this Man works many signs. If we let Him alone like this everyone will believe in Him, and the Romans will come and take away both our place and nation."

The high priest Caiaphas reproaches them. "You know nothing at all," he fumes. "Nor do you consider that it is expedient for us that one man should die for the people, and not that the whole nation should perish." He thus unwittingly announces, in a moment of profound, world-historical irony, the saving power of Jesus' death for the nation. "And not for the nation only," John writes, "but also that He would gather together in one the children of God who were scattered abroad." The council begins to plot Jesus' death, and Jesus withdraws to Ephraim with His disciples because He can no longer travel openly.

51   EPHRAIM TO JERUSALEM VIA SAMARIA, GALILEE, AND PEREA

Ten Lepers

◀ Luke 17:11-37

Though on His way to Jerusalem, Jesus travels north through Samaria, and Galilee, where He encounters a group of ten lepers who stand "afar off" crying, "Jesus, Master, have mercy on us!"

"Go show yourselves to the priests," Jesus commands them. As they go, they are cleansed. One of the ten, a Samaritan, cries out in a loud voice, glorifying God. He returns to Jesus falling down on his face at His feet, thanking Him. "Were there not ten cleansed?" Jesus asks. "Where are the other nine? . . . Were there not any found who returned to give glory to God except this foreigner?" He then commends the one: "Arise, go your way. Your faith has made you well."

Asked by certain Pharisees when the kingdom of God will come, Jesus counters that "the kingdom of God is within you." He points out that "the kingdom of God does not come with observation." "Nor will they say, 'See here!' or 'See there!'"

Turning to His disciples He announces that the time is approaching when they will long "to see one of the days of the Son of Man" but will not see it. He continues that His second coming will be like lightning flashing from one end of the sky to the other. In that day, the people will be unprepared for the impending judgment, just as they were in Noah's day before the flood and in Lot's day at the judgment of Sodom and Gomorrah.

"They ate, they drank, they married wives, they were given in marriage, until the day that Noah entered the ark, and the flood came and destroyed them all," Jesus says. "Likewise as it was also in the days of Lot, they bought, they sold, they planted, they built; but on the day that Lot went out of Sodom it rained fire and brimstone from heaven and destroyed them all." In the "day that the Son of Man is revealed" there will be two women grinding together, or "two men will be in the field." One will be taken up and the other left behind. "Where, Lord?" His disciples ask. "Wherever the body is, there the vultures will gather," Jesus replies.

The Importunate Widow

Luke 18:1-14 ▶

In a parable instructing His disciples to pray without losing heart, Jesus tells of an importunate widow who goes day after day to petition a judge who neither fears God nor regards men. "Get justice for me from my adversary," she entreats him. The judge refuses her for a time but relents in the end. "Because this woman troubles me I will avenge her, lest by her continual coming she weary me," he decides. "Hear what the unjust judge said," Jesus advises His disciples. "Shall not God avenge His own elect who cry out day and night to Him? I tell you that He will avenge them speedily." But "when the Son of Man comes," Jesus wonders, "will He really find faith on the earth?"

In a parable directed at those "who trusted in themselves that they were righteous and despised others," He tells of two men who go to the Temple to pray. The first is a self-righteous Pharisee. "God, I thank you that I am not like other men—extortioners, unjust, adulterers, or even as this tax collector," he says, indicating the other man. He then proudly recounts his good deeds to God. The tax collector "standing afar off, would not so much as raise his eyes to heaven" as he "beat his breast, saying, 'God, be merciful to me a sinner!'" Of the two men it is the tax collector that returns to his house justified, Jesus says. "For everyone who exalts himself will be humbled, and he who humbles himself will be exalted."

Instruction on Divorce

Matthew 19:1-12 ▶
Mark 10:1-12 ▶

Large crowds follow Jesus as He nears Judea beyond the Jordan. He teaches and heals them there, as is His custom. "Is it lawful for a man to divorce his wife for just any reason?" the Pharisees ask, hoping to entrap Him. Jesus answers that a husband and wife "are no longer two but one flesh." In that case, "what God has joined together let no man separate."

"Why then did Moses command to give a certificate of divorce and to put her away?" they counter. Here they refer for the sake of argument to provisions in the Mosaic Law for divorce under certain conditions (see Deuteronomy 24:1). Jesus tells them that Moses "permitted you to divorce your wives" because of "the hardness of your hearts." He then draws the line hard and fast: "I say to you, whoever divorces his wife except for sexual immorality, and marries another, commits adultery; and whoever marries her who is divorced commits adultery."

The disciples reason that, if the commandment concerning divorce is as inflexible as that, "it is better not to marry." Jesus rejoins that not everyone is cut out for the life of sexual continence, "but only those to whom it has been given." The sense is that celibacy is a spiritual gift or charisma. "He who is able to accept it, let him accept it," Jesus tells them.

Jesus Welcomes the Children

At this point the synoptic Gospels give an account of people bringing little children to Jesus "that He might put His hands on them and pray." The disciples rebuke the people, drawing Jesus' ire on themselves. "Let the little children come to Me, and do not forbid them," Jesus says, "greatly displeased" and taking the children up in His arms. He touches them and blesses them. "Whoever does not receive the kingdom of God as a little child will by no means enter it," He warns.

◄ Matthew 19:13-15
◄ Mark 10:13-16
◄ Luke 18:15-17

The Rich Young Ruler

On the road to Jerusalem a young man comes running and kneels before him. "Good Teacher," he says to Jesus, "what good thing shall I do that I may have eternal life?" "Why do you call me good?" Jesus asks him. "No one is good but One . . . You know the commandments." "Teacher, all these things I have kept from my youth," the young man protests. Mark writes that Jesus, "looking at him, loved him."

◄ Matthew 19:16–20
◄ Mark 10:17-31
◄ Luke 18:18-30

"One thing you lack," Jesus tells him, "sell whatever you have and give to the poor" then "come, take up the cross, and follow me." The young man is suddenly crestfallen, since he is very rich and "had great possessions." Seeing "that he became sorrowful," Jesus looks around at His disciples. "Children, how hard it is for those who trust in riches to enter the kingdom of God!" It would be "easier for a camel to go through the eye of a needle." The disciples are "greatly astonished." "'Who then can be saved?'" they reply. "With God," Jesus assures them, "all things are possible."

"See, we have left all and followed You," Peter reminds Jesus. "Therefore, what shall we have?" Jesus confirms that they will indeed be rewarded. "There is no one who has left house or brothers or sisters or father or mother or wife or children or lands" who will not be rewarded. In addition to eternal life in the world to come, they may expect to receive "a hundred-fold now in this time," with plenty of persecutions to boot.

Jesus tells them the story of a landowner who hires workers for his vineyard at 6:00 A.M. He goes back out at 9:00 A.M., 12:00 P.M., and 3:00 P.M. to hire more laborers, and finally again at 5:00 P.M. he hires on some stragglers. At 6:00 P.M., when it is time to pay everyone, those hired at 5:00 P.M. get paid first, and receive a full day's wage. The workers who have been there all day assume they will be paid more, but they, too, get only a day's pay. When they complain of unfair treatment they are rebuffed by the landlord who points out that they were paid the agreed wage and that he as the owner of his own money is free to be generous to whomever he will.

A Request From James and John

Matthew 20:17-28 ▶
Mark 10:32-45 ▶
Luke 18:31-34 ▶

As they get closer to Jerusalem, Jesus tells His disciples that He is about to be "betrayed to the chief priests and scribes," condemned, handed over to the Gentiles, mocked, scourged, spat at, and crucified; but that He will be raised from the dead on the third day. This is the third prediction by Jesus of His impending death. The disciples understand none of this.

The brothers James and John seize this inopportune moment to solicit a favor from Him. "Teacher, we want You to do for us whatever we ask," they say. "What do you want me to do?" Jesus asks. "Grant us that we may sit, one on Your right hand and the other on Your left, in Your glory," they answer. "Are you able to drink the cup that I am about to drink?" Jesus says. "We are able," the brothers glibly reply. In that case, "you will indeed drink My cup," Jesus assures them. Unfortunately for them, the places of honor in heaven are "not Mine to give."

When the disciples hear that James and John are trying to secure honors in heaven, they are indignant. Jesus calls them all together, explaining that while "the rulers of the Gentiles lord it over them" it "shall not be so among you." Rather, "whoever desires to be first among you, let him be your slave—just as the Son of Man did not come to be served but to serve, and to give His life a ransom for many."

52   PEREA TO JERICHO

The Healing of Blind Bartimaeus

Matthew 20:29-34 ▶
Mark 10:46-52 ▶
Luke 18:35-43 ▶

As they pass out of Perea and cross the Jordan River heading for Jericho, the group passes a blind man named Bartimaeus, begging on the side of the road (Matthew indicates that there were two blind beggars). Hearing the multitude passing by, Bartimaeus asks what it means. The people tell him that it is Jesus of Nazareth. At this the beggar cries out, "Jesus, Son of David, have mercy on me!" The people try to shut him up, but he cries more insistently still. Jesus pauses and asks that the man be brought to Him. "What do you want Me to do for you?" Jesus asks Him. "Rabboni, that I may receive my sight," Bartimaeus answers. "Go your way," Jesus tells him, "your faith has made you well." The man is instantly healed and "followed Him, glorifying God."

The Salvation of Zacchaeus

Luke 19:1-28 ▶

In Jericho, a rich tax collector named Zacchaeus is prevented by his short stature from seeing above the crowd. Hoping to catch a glimpse of Jesus the resourceful man races ahead of the crowd and scrambles up a sycamore tree for a better view. Jesus spots Zacchaeus in the tree. "Zacchaeus," Jesus calls to him from beneath the tree, "make haste and come down, for today I must stay at your house." Zacchaeus hurries down and receives Him with joy.

The people grumble that Jesus "has gone to be a guest of a man who is a sinner." Standing in their midst, Zacchaeus announces, "Look, Lord, I give half of my goods to the poor; and if I have taken anything from anyone by false accusation, I restore fourfold."

"Today salvation has come to this house," Jesus tells those assembled, "for the Son of Man has come to seek and to save that which was lost." Here Jesus delivers a parable to counter the people's expectation that the kingdom of God is about to appear. In the parable, a ruler leaves for a foreign country to receive a kingdom and then return. In his absence, he leaves a large sum of money with each of ten servants to do business with until he returns. After he leaves, his citizens send a delegation after him to say that they do not want him to rule over them.

When the ruler returns, his servants come before him to account for their stewardship of his assets. One has increased his money ten times, another five. The master rewards them with cities to rule over, ten and five respectively. Yet another of his servants has hidden his money in the ground, hoping thus to keep from losing it. The ruler angrily confiscates the money from him and gives it to one of his more faithful servants. He then has the citizens who opposed him brought before him and executed. After delivering this parable Jesus moves on, headed for Jerusalem via Bethany.

53 JERICHO TO BETHANY

Arrival in Bethany

◀ John 11:55–12:1, 9-11

Passover is just six days away. It is one of three annual feasts Jewish males are commanded by law to celebrate in Jerusalem. The people begin to arrive in Jerusalem, wondering among themselves whether Jesus will come, since the religious leaders hope to arrest Him and put Him to death. The chief priests and the Pharisees have given orders that anyone who sees Him must report Him. When the people learn that Jesus is in Bethany, they travel there to see Him and His friend who has come back from the dead. There are so many coming to believe in Jesus because of this resurrection that the religious leaders decide to have Lazarus executed as well.

Conclusion

Jesus' teaching is a crucial aspect of His ministry to the Twelve. Luke records parables dealing with entrance into the kingdom, salvation and God's love for sinners, stewardship and the cost of discipleship, prayer, and divorce. The raising of Lazarus from the dead is an extremely important lesson for the disciples, who must soon grapple with Jesus' own death and resurrection.

Passion Week: Sunday – Wednesday

Jesus enters Jerusalem for what has come to be known as His Passion Week. Here He brings the objectives of His earthly life to their climax. This chapter will take us through the first part of the week, beginning with His reception as He rides into Jerusalem. Also recorded are His last, crucial instructions to His disciples and His final battles with the religious leaders.

Spring, A.D. 30

54 BACK AND FORTH FROM BETHANY TO JERUSALEM

Sunday

Triumphal Entry

On Sunday Jesus departs Bethany for Jerusalem. At Bethphage He sends two of His disciples into a village to borrow a donkey (two donkeys, in Matthew's account): "Go into the village," Jesus instructs. There "you will find a colt tied, on which no one has sat. Loose it and bring it here." The disciples find the colt but as they are unloosing it, its owners confront them. "Why are you loosing the colt?" they ask. "The Lord has need of him," the disciples answer as Jesus instructed them.

◄ Matthew 21:1-11,14-17
◄ Mark 11:1-11
◄ Luke 19:29-44
◄ John 12:12-19

The disciples lay their clothing on the animal and set Jesus upon it. As the colt approaches the city of Jerusalem, a great multitude gathers, spreading their garments and leafy branches cut from the trees in the road before Him. This historic entrance to the city is foretold centuries earlier in the book of the prophet Zechariah who writes: "Rejoice greatly, O daughter of Zion . . . Behold your King is coming to you . . . lowly, and riding on a donkey, a colt, the foal of a donkey" (Zechariah 9:9).

The crowds lining the road cry a salutation derived from Psalm 118: "Hosanna to the son of David! Blessed is He who comes in the name of the Lord!" (*Hosanna* being the Hebrew equivalent of the English phrase *save us*). Matthew writes that as Jesus enters Jerusalem, "all the city was moved, saying, 'Who is this?'"

"This is Jesus, the prophet from Nazareth of Galilee," the triumphal crowd replies. John writes that many of these people were with Him when He raised Lazarus from the dead and "bore witness" compelling others to accept the testimony of this sign. Some of the Pharisees present at this outpouring of messianic anticipation call to Jesus from the crowd. "Teacher, rebuke your disciples," they adjure Him. "If these should be quiet," Jesus answers, "the stones would immediately cry out."

"You see that you are accomplishing nothing," the Pharisees bicker at one another. "Look, the world has gone after Him." As Jesus draws near to the city He begins to weep. "Days will come upon you," Jesus laments, "when your enemies will build an embankment around you, surround you and close you in on every side and level you and your children within you." They will "not leave in you one stone upon another, because you did not know the time of your visitation."

Jesus soon arrives at the Temple where the blind and lame gather. Here He heals them. When the chief priests and scribes see "the wonderful things that He did" and hear the children in the Temple crying out, "Hosanna to the Son of David!" they are indignant. "Do you hear what these are saying?" they demand. "Have you never read?" Jesus replies, producing a psalm of King David: "Out of the mouths of babes and nursing infants You have perfected praise" (see Psalm 8:2). Later He returns with the Twelve from Jerusalem to Bethany where He will spend the night, "as the hour was already late."

Cursing the Fig Tree and Cleansing the Temple

Monday
Matthew 21:12-13, 18-19 ▶
Mark 11:12-18 ▶
Luke 19:45-48 ▶

Returning with His disciples to the Temple on Monday, Jesus sees "from afar a fig tree having leaves" and so approaches it to "see if perhaps He would find something on it." Finding no fruit on it, Jesus says to the tree, "Let no one eat fruit from you ever again."

Upon their arrival in the Temple, Jesus drives out those found buying and selling in its premises, overthrowing the money changers' tables and the seats of the dove traders. He repeats His earlier rebuke. "It is written," Jesus announces, citing the prophet Isaiah, "My house is a house of prayer" (see Isaiah 56:7). "But you have made it a den of thieves," He adds, deploying a line from the prophet Jeremiah (see Jeremiah 7:11).

Discourse on His Death

John 12:20-50 ▶

Some Greeks who have come to worship at the feast ask Philip to introduce them to Jesus. Philip alerts Andrew, and the two take the request to Jesus. "The hour is come," Jesus says, "that the Son of Man should be glorified." "He who loves his life will lose it, and he who hates his life in this world will keep it for eternal life." Illustrating His point with an image drawn from the natural world, Jesus tells His disciples that "unless a grain of wheat falls into the ground and dies, it remains alone; but if it dies, it produces much grain."

"My soul is troubled," Jesus says. "What shall I say? 'Father, save me from this hour'? But for this purpose I came to this hour." Rather than demand to be spared, He bows to His Father's will. "Father, glorify your name," He prays.

At this "a voice came from heaven saying, **'I have both glorified it, and will glorify it again.'**" Some in the crowd claim to hear thunder, others decide, "an angel has spoken to Him."

"The voice did not come because of Me," Jesus tells them, "but for your sake." He warns the people that "the judgment of this world has come" and that its ruler will soon be cast out. Prefiguring His own death and its redemptory effect, Jesus assures His listeners that "if I am lifted up from the earth, [I] will draw all peoples to Myself."

The crowds protest these predictions: "How can You say that 'the Son of Man must be lifted up?'" they demand. "We have heard from the law that the Christ remains forever." Just "who is this Son of Man?"

"A little while longer the light is with you," Jesus tells them, ignoring their questions and striking a further note of warning. "Walk while you have the light, lest darkness overtake you." The time for repentance and conversion is waning. "While you have the light, believe in the light, that you may become sons of light," Jesus urges His listeners.

John writes that, "although He had done so many signs before them, they did not believe in Him." "Who has believed our report? And to whom has the arm of the Lord been revealed?" the prophet Isaiah laments (see Isaiah 53:1). Rather, God has Himself "blinded their eyes and hardened their hearts, lest they should see with their eyes, lest they should understand with their hearts and turn" and be healed (see Isaiah 6:10). The Gospel writer reveals that "these things Isaiah said when he saw His glory and spoke of Him" centuries before His rejection at Jerusalem. Even among Israel's leaders there are at this moment many that have come to believe in Him, "but because of the Pharisees they did not confess Him, lest they should be put out of the synagogue."

Jesus' final words to the crowd take the form of a challenge. "I have come as a light into the world, that whoever believes in Me should not abide in darkness." "He who rejects Me [will be judged] in the last day [by] the word that I have spoken."

"I have not spoken on My own authority," Jesus assures His listeners. Rather, "the Father who sent Me gave Me a command, what I should say and what I should speak. And I know that His command is everlasting life."

Withered Fig Tree

As Jesus and the disciples head from the city that evening, they pass the fig tree Jesus cursed. The disciples are stunned to see the tree has withered away to its roots. "Rabbi, look!" Peter exclaims. "Whatever things you ask when you pray," Jesus answers him, "believe that you receive them, and you will have them." Furthermore, "whenever you stand praying, if you have anything against anyone, forgive him."

◀ Matthew 21:19-22
◀ Mark 11:19-25
◀ Luke 21:37-38

Tuesday
Matthew 21:23–22:14 ▶
Mark 11:27–12:12 ▶
Luke 20:1-19 ▶

Parables Against the Religious Leaders

The next day, Jesus returns to the Temple where the priests, scribes, and elders confront Him. "Tell us, by what authority are You doing these things?" they demand. "I also will ask you one thing," Jesus replies. "Answer me and I will tell you by what authority I do these things. The baptism of John—was it from heaven or from men?"

"If we say 'From heaven,' He will say, 'Why then did you not believe him?'" the Pharisees reason. "But if we say, 'From men,' all the people will stone us, for they are persuaded that John was a prophet." "We do not know," they answer. "Neither will I tell you by what authority I do these things," Jesus replies.

"But what do you think?" He asks them. "A man had two sons." Their father approaches each of them with a request to "go work in my vineyard." The first son answers, "I will not go," but later regrets his refusal and goes out to the vineyard. The second son assures his father, "I go, sir" but then reneges. "Which of the two did the will of his father?" Jesus asks the Pharisees. The leaders answer that it is undoubtedly the son who repented and worked. "Assuredly, I say to you," Jesus says, "tax collectors and harlots enter the kingdom of God before you." "For John came to you in the way of righteousness and you did not believe him; but tax collectors and harlots believed him."

"Hear another parable," Jesus says. This one is about a man who plants a vineyard, outfitting it with a winepress and tower and setting a hedge around it. He then leases it to certain vinedressers before leaving for a far country. When the owner sends a servant to collect from them the harvest at vintage-time, he is beaten and sent away empty handed. A second envoy is stoned. Him they wounded in the head and sent back "shamefully treated." Yet another is killed. Many others deputized by their master to collect the harvest suffer thus at the hands of the mutinous vinedressers. Finally, the owner sends his son, thinking that he will be respected and heeded, but when the vinedressers see the son they conspire among themselves: "This is the heir. Come, let us kill him and seize his inheritance." The son is then cast out of the vineyard and killed. "When the owner of the vineyard comes," Jesus asks, "what will he do to those vinedressers?"

"He will destroy those wicked men miserably," the leaders insist. Furthermore he "will lease his vineyard to other vinedressers who will render to him the fruits in their seasons." "Therefore I say to you," Jesus explains, "the kingdom of God will be taken from you and given to a nation bearing the fruits of it.

"Have you never read in the Scriptures," He asks, "'the stone which the builders rejected has become the chief cornerstone. This was the Lord's doing, and it is marvelous in our eyes'?" The reference is from Psalm 118 and is no doubt familiar to His listeners who realize that Jesus has spoken the parable against them. "Whoever falls on this stone will be broken," Jesus says. "But on whomever it falls, it will grind him to powder."

A third parable concerns a king who prepares a marriage feast for his son and sends his servants to collect the invited guests. The ungrateful guests refuse to come. He sends other servants, but they are likewise ignored and even beaten and killed. In his anger the king sends his army to destroy those invited, and then sends his servants into the surrounding area to invite all they can find both bad and good so that the wedding hall is filled. At the feast, the king finds among these hastily assembled guests a man not dressed for the wedding. "Bind him hand and foot, take him away and cast him into the outer darkness," the king instructs his servants. "For many are called," Jesus explains, "but few are chosen."

Question Concerning Taxation

The Pharisees regroup and send some of their disciples, posing as upright men, to ensnare Jesus by asking Him a loaded question about taxation. They hope to implicate Him in a political dispute concerning Israel's relationship to the ruling authorities in Rome. "Teacher, we know that You are true and teach the way of God in truth," they blandish Him. "Nor do You care about anyone, for You do not regard the person of men. Tell us, therefore, what do You think?" The question has to do with whether or not it is lawful according to the Torah to pay taxes to Caesar. "Why do you test Me, you hypocrites? Show me the tax money." The men produce a Roman denarius. "Whose image and inscription is this?" "Caesar's," they answer. "Render therefore to Caesar the things that are Caesar's," Jesus replies, "and to God the things that are God's." His questioners marvel that Jesus has thus neatly evaded their trap.

◀ Matthew 22:15-22
◀ Mark 12:13-17
◀ Luke 20:20-26

Jesus Silences the Sadducees

Seeing that the Pharisees are unable to silence Jesus, the Sadducees confront Him with a story of a married man who died and whose brother then married the widow in keeping with the Law (see Deuteronomy 25:5-10). The second man died, and a third brother took his place, and so on with all seven brothers. The question is this: whose wife will the woman be in the resurrection? This is a curious question coming from the Sadducees, who repudiate the notion of a resurrection from the dead. In fact it reveals their unfaith together with the ridicule in which they hold all such belief.

◀ Matthew 22:23-33
◀ Mark 12:18-27
◀ Luke 20:27-40

By this hypothetical case they hope to involve Jesus in a logical contradiction discrediting Him. "You are mistaken," Jesus tells them, "not knowing the Scriptures nor the power of God. For in the resurrection they neither marry nor are given in marriage, but are like the angels of God in heaven." He rebukes the Sadducees for their incomprehension and disbelief. "Have you not read what was spoken to you by God, saying, '**I *am* the God of Abraham, the God of Isaac, and the God of Jacob**?' God is not the God of the dead, but of the living."

Matthew 22:34-40 ▶
Mark 12:28-34 ▶

Two Great Commandments

The Pharisees resume the attack, seeing an opportunity as teachers of the Law to entrap Jesus with a question about legal priority. "Teacher, which is the greatest commandment in the law?" a lawyer from among them asks. Jesus states flatly that the greatest commandment is to love God. He is referring here to the Shema, a passage from the Torah in which the people of Israel are commanded thus: "Hear, O Israel: the Lord our God, the Lord is one! You shall love the Lord your God with all your heart, with all your soul, and with all your strength" (Deuteronomy 6:4-5). "This is the first and great commandment," Jesus tells them.

The second greatest commandment is similar to the first: "You shall love your neighbor as yourself" (see Leviticus 19:18). "On these two commandments hang all the Law and the Prophets."

Matthew 22:41-46 ▶
Mark 12:35-37 ▶
Luke 20:41-44 ▶

Jesus Confounds the Pharisees

Jesus then turns the tables on the Pharisees' pretensions to authority in matters concerning the Law. "What do you think about the Christ?" Jesus queries them. "Whose son is He?" "The Son of David," the Pharisees answer. This is a point on which there is unanimous agreement, as the Davidic lineage of the Messiah is amply testified by the Scriptures. "How then does David in the Spirit call Him 'Lord,' saying: The Lord said to my Lord, 'Sit at my right hand, till I make Your enemies Your footstool'?"

The question is difficult, even baffling, since it is believed that in this reference from Psalm 110, God beckons to His throne the Messiah, whom David himself addresses as 'Lord.' Why would King David apply to his own son the honorific 'Lord'? The question may not be unanswerable, given what we know about Jesus' divine generation, but it confounds the Pharisees. They are so nonplussed by this christological riddle that from this day on no one "dared question Him anymore."

Peter will later adduce this same reference from Psalm 110 when arguing that "God has made this Jesus whom you crucified both Lord and Christ" (Acts 2:36). It is clearer than ever after Jesus' death and ascension that He was in terms of human parentage the Son of David but David's Lord in His exaltation to God's right hand.

Matthew 23:1-39 ▶
Mark 12:38-40 ▶
Luke 20:45-47 ▶

Denunciation of the Scribes and Pharisees

Jesus warns the crowds in the strongest language yet of the deceitfulness of their scribes and Pharisees by issuing a series of anathemas against their conduct as leaders. He acknowledges that in holding the "seat of Moses," the leaders deserve the people's respect: "Whatever they tell you to observe, that observe and do," Jesus instructs. "But do not do according to their works," He warns them.

"All their works they do to be seen by men." They love to dress pompously and take "the best places at the feasts, the best seats in the synagogues, greetings in the marketplaces, and to be called by men, 'Rabbi, Rabbi.'" Jesus' followers are to shun such honors: "But you, do not be called 'Rabbi'; for One is your teacher, the Christ, and you are all brethren . . . He who is greatest among you shall be your servant. And whoever exalts himself will be humbled."

"Woe to you scribes and Pharisees, hypocrites!" Jesus says. "You shut up the kingdom of heaven against men," you neither enter "nor do you allow those who are entering it to go in."For this they will themselves recieve the "greater condemnation."

The pitch and intensity of Jesus' rebuke mounts."You devour widows' houses, and for a pretense make long prayers." Though "you travel land and sea" to win a single convert, "when he is won, you make him twice as much a son of hell as yourselves." For true obedience to God's word these leaders have substitued a convoluted system of legalistic interpretations and subtle but meaningless distinctions. "Woe to you, blind guides, who say 'Whoever swears by the temple, it is nothing; but whoever swears by the gold of the temple, he is obliged to perform it.'"

"Fools and blind! For which is greater, the gold or the temple that sanctifies the gold?" There are those too "who say 'Whoever swears by the altar, it is nothing; but whoever swears by the gift that is on it, he is obliged to perform it.'"

"Fools and blind!" Jesus scoffs. "For which is greater, the gift or the altar that sanctifies the gift?" Rather, to swear by the altar is to swear "by all things on it." Swearing by the Temple is the same as swearing by "Him who dwells in it." Finally, "he who swears by heaven, swears by the throne of God and by Him who sits on it."

Scrupulous in the tithing of their spices, "mint and anise and cumin," the scribes and Pharisees have "neglected the weightier matters of the law: justice and mercy and faith. These you ought to have done without leaving the others undone," Jesus says. "Blind guides, who strain out a gnat and swallow a camel!"

"Woe to you scribes and Pharisees, hypocrites! For you cleanse the outside of the cup and dish" when it is brimming with self-indulgence and extortion. "Blind Pharisee, first cleanse the inside of the cup and dish, that the outside of them may be clean also."

"Woe to you scribes and Pharisees, hypocrites!" Like "whitewashed tombs which indeed appear beautiful outwardly" you house "dead men's bones and all uncleanness" within. Posing as righteous men, "inside you are filled with hypocrisy and lawlessness."

Building tombs and adorning monuments to righteous men, the scribes and Pharisees congratulate themselves: "If we had lived in the days of our fathers, we would not have" joined with them in shedding "the blood of the prophets." Jesus charges that their own words stand evidence against them, since they are indeed the sons and heirs of those who murdered the prophets. "Serpents, brood of vipers! How can you escape the condemnation of hell?"

"O Jerusalem, Jerusalem, the one who kills the prophets and stones those who are sent to her," Jesus laments. "How often I wanted to gather your children together, as a hen gathers her chicks under her wings, but you were not willing! See! Your house is left to you desolate!"

The Widow's Mite

Mark 12:41-44 ▶
Luke 21:1-4 ▶

As Jesus watches people in the Temple treasury putting money into the offering, He points out to His disciples a widow who has deposited just two mites. He tells them that "this poor widow has put in more than all who have given to the treasury; for they put in out of their abundance, but she out of her poverty put in all that she had, her whole livelihood. Notwithstanding Jesus' repeated warnings and prophetic announcements, His disciples seem to have little idea of what will transpire over the next few days.

55 FROM THE TEMPLE TO THE MOUNT OF OLIVES

Mount of Olives Discourse

Matthew 24:1–25:46 ▶
Mark 13:1-37 ▶
Luke 21:5-36 ▶

Jesus departs the Temple for the last time and heads for the top of the Mount of Olives, where His disciples comment on the Temple's beauty. Jesus replies that not one stone of it will be left standing on another. As they sit together on the mount, the four fishermen—Peter, James, John, and Andrew—ask Jesus when this destruction will take place, prompting a lengthy discourse from Jesus on the events surrounding His second coming.

Jesus does not give His disciples the exact time of His return, but describes many of the events that will precede it:

● False prophets and messiahs will come and lead many astray.

● There will be wars and rumors of wars.

● Earthquakes and famine will occur.

● Believers will be delivered over to religious and civil authorities.

● Families will be divided and turn against one another.

● The Gospel will be preached to the whole world.

- The "abomination of desolation" prophesied by Daniel will stand in the Temple.

- Jerusalem will be surrounded by the armies of her enemies.

Jesus forewarns His disciples of these things so they will not be deceived when false prophets arise. He assures them that His coming will be as swift as lightning flashing across the sky. The heavens will be shaken, the sun will be darkened, and the moon will not give its light. The stars will fall from heaven. "Then they will see the Son of Man coming," Jesus tells them, "in the clouds with great power and glory." He will send out His angels to "gather together His elect from the four winds, from the farthest part of earth to the farthest part of heaven."

He then delivers a series of parables to teach His disciples to be prepared for His return:

- The parable of the fig tree is a warning to pay attention to the signs of His coming. As in the days of Noah, when those who ignored the signs of God's judgment died in the flood, many will ignore the signs of His return and be left behind.

- The parable of the faithful servant and the evil servant teaches that the faithful disciple of Jesus is the one who is found doing God's work when He returns. The evil servant takes advantage of his master's absence to follow his own evil desires and is punished when his master returns at an unexpected hour.

- The parable of the ten virgins teaches the importance of being prepared for Jesus' return, and warns that those who are unprepared are in danger of being excluded from His wedding feast.

- The parable of the talents teaches us that we will all be held accountable for the investment of the resources God has entrusted to us. Those who invest their resources in the building of God's kingdom will be rewarded, while those who do nothing will suffer loss.

- The parable of the sheep and goats represents the final judgment that will separate the faithful from the unfaithful.

Leaders Conspire to Kill Jesus

◀ Matthew 26:1-5
◀ Mark 14:1-2
◀ Luke 22:1-2

Jesus and His disciples return to Bethany Tuesday evening after His teaching concerning the end of time. Here He tells His followers that He will be crucified during the Passover, just two days hence. This constitutes Jesus' fourth prediction of imminent suffering and death. Meanwhile, the chief priest Caiaphas plots with the other leaders to kill Him.

Anointing for Burial

◀ Matthew 26:6-13
◀ Mark 14:3-9
◀ John 12:2-8

That evening Jesus has dinner with His disciples at the house of Simon the leper. Also present are Lazarus, Mary, and Martha. During the evening, Mary anoints Jesus' feet with a "very costly oil of spikenard." She wipes His feet with her hair as the fragrance of the oil fills the house. This prompts a complaint from Judas Iscariot: "Why was this fragrant oil not sold for three hundred denarii and given to the poor?" John writes that Judas complains not from a concern for the poor but because he kept the money box and helped himself to its contents. "Let her alone," Jesus rebukes Judas. "The poor you have with you always, but Me you do not always have." He commends Mary since she "has come beforehand to anoint My body for burial." For this good work she will be remembered "wherever this gospel is preached in the whole world."

Judas' Betrayal

Matthew 26:14-16 ▶
Mark 14:10-11 ▶
Luke 22:3-6 ▶

At this rebuke from Jesus, Judas goes to the chief priests and captains. "What are you willing to give me if I deliver Him to you?" he offers. Luke writes that "Satan had entered Judas, surnamed Iscariot," inciting him to this act of betrayal. The chief priests are only too glad to purchase for an ally one of the Twelve and "counted out for him 30 pieces of silver." The deal cemented, Judas begins plotting a way to conveniently betray Him.

Wednesday

Wednesday is a day of rest for Jesus and His disciples in Bethany. The Bible records no activity on this day.

Conclusion

Jesus has now cleansed the Temple for the final time. He has weathered the verbal attacks of His opponents, silencing them all, and has given His last public teaching. Anointed for His burial, and betrayed by Judas, the consummation of His earthly ministry is at hand.

PASSION WEEK ITINERARY

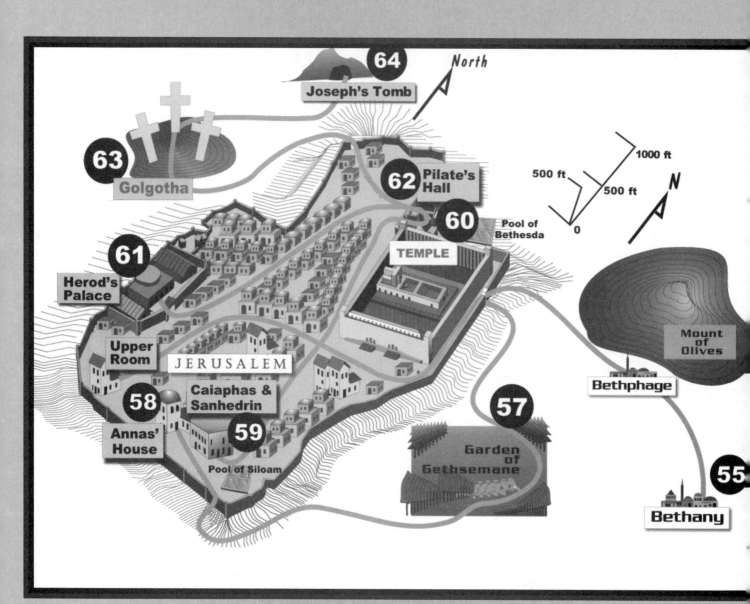

Passion Week: Thursday – Saturday

This chapter will cover the Passover meal, the Upper Room Discourse, the trial, condemnation, crucifixion, and burial of Jesus.

56 BETHANY BACK TO JERUSALEM (UPPER ROOM)

Thursday

Preparation for the Passover Meal

On Thursday Jesus and His disciples prepare for the eight days of Passover that will begin at sunset. This feast is an annual reenactment of the dramatic Exodus of the Israelites from slavery in Egypt and a celebration of God's deliverance by the blood of the Passover lamb.

"Where do you want us to go and prepare, that You may eat the Passover?" the disciples ask Jesus. Jesus tells Peter and John to go into the city where a man carrying a pitcher of water on his head will meet them. They are to follow him home and ask the master of the house for the guest room in which to eat the Passover meal. The owner will "show you to a large, furnished upper room . . . There make ready," Jesus tells them.

◀ Matthew 26:17-19
◀ Mark 14:12-16
◀ Luke 22:7-13

The Last Supper

When evening comes, Jesus brings the disciples together in the Upper Room. "With fervent desire," Jesus says, "I have desired to eat this Passover with you before I suffer." Over supper Jesus addresses a dispute between His disciples about who among them will be considered the greatest. He reminds them that while the Gentiles measure greatness by their authority over others it will "not be so among you."

"On the contrary," Jesus assures them, the standard for greatness among them must be a standard of servanthood. He promises to bestow upon them "a kingdom, just as My Father bestowed one upon Me," but reminds them that he who governs must be as he who serves, just as "I am among you as the One who serves."

◀ Matthew 26:20
◀ Mark 14:17
◀ Luke 22:14-16, 24-30

Washing the Disciples' Feet

During the meal, Jesus rises from the table, takes a basin of water and a towel and begins to wash the disciples' feet. When He approaches Simon Peter, the disciple balks, "Lord, are you washing my feet?" "What I am doing you do not understand now," Jesus tells him. "You

◀ John 13:1-20

shall never wash my feet!" Peter vows. "If I do not wash you, you have no part of me," Jesus says. In that case "not my feet only, but also my hands and my head," Peter replies. "You are clean," Jesus assures him, "but not all of you." By this He indicates His foreknowledge of betrayal at the hands of Judas Iscariot.

"You call me Teacher and Lord, and you say well, for so I am," Jesus says to His disciples, taking His seat at the table. "If I then, your Lord and Teacher, have washed your feet, you also ought to wash one another's feet. For I have given you an example, that you should do as I have done to you. Most assuredly, I say to you, a servant is not greater than his master." Jesus then indicates that His betrayer is among them, "that the Scripture may be fulfilled, 'He who eats bread with Me has lifted up his heel against me'" (see Psalm 41:9).

The Revelation of the Betrayer

Matthew 26:21-25 ▶
Mark 14:18-21 ▶
Luke 22:21-23 ▶
John 13:21-30 ▶

"One of you is going to betray me," Jesus says. The disciples are grieved to hear it and look at one another, "perplexed about whom He spoke." "Lord, is it I?" they begin asking. Peter motions to John who is seated beside Jesus to find out who He means. "Lord, who is it?" John inquires. "It is he to whom I shall give this piece of bread," Jesus replies. He then hands the piece to Judas Iscariot. "Rabbi, is it I?" Judas asks. "You have said it," Jesus says. "What you do, do quickly."

John writes that "having received the piece of bread, he went out immediately. And it was night." The other disciples are unsure of what is happening until later in the evening. "The Son of Man indeed goes just as it is written of Him," Jesus says, "but woe to that man by whom the Son of Man is betrayed! It would have been good for that man if he had never been born."

Jesus' Warning About Desertion

Matthew 26:31-35 ▶
Mark 14:27-31 ▶
Luke 22:31-38 ▶
John 13:31-38 ▶

Jesus reminds them that the hour of His glorification has drawn near and that love is the sign of true discipleship. "Little children, I shall be with you a little while longer," He says. "Where I am going you cannot come."

"Lord," Simon Peter answers, "why can I not follow You now? I will lay down my life for You." "Will you lay down your life for My sake?" Jesus asks. "Most assuredly I say to you, the rooster shall not crow till you have denied Me three times."

"All of you will be made to stumble because of Me this night," Jesus tells them, citing a passage from the Old Testament prophet Zechariah which reads, "Strike the shepherd and the sheep will be scattered" (Zechariah 13:7). He explains this Scripture as a foretokening of their desertion later that evening. Peter protests his loyalty: "Even if all are made to stumble, yet I will not be." "If I have to die with You," he assures Jesus, "I will not deny You." Mark adds that the rest of the disciples "all said likewise."

New Covenant Instituted

◀ Matthew 26:26-29
◀ Mark 14:22-25
◀ Luke 22:17-20
◀ 1 Corinthians 11:23-26

At this point in the meal, Jesus institutes the New Covenant foretold by the prophet Jeremiah centuries earlier:

> Behold the days are coming, says the Lord, when I will make a new covenant with the house of Israel and with the house of Judah—not according to the covenant that I made with their fathers in the day that I took them by the hand to lead them out of the land of Egypt, My covenant which they broke, though I was a husband to them, says the Lord. But this is the covenant that I will make with the house of Israel after those days, says the Lord: I will put My law in their minds, and write it on their hearts; and I will be their God, and they shall be My people. No more shall every man teach his neighbor, and every man his brother, saying, "Know the Lord," for they all shall know Me, from the least of them to the greatest of them, says the Lord. For I will forgive their iniquity, and their sin I will remember no more.
>
> — Jeremiah 31:31-34

Under the New Covenant the meaning of the Passover celebration is broadened and fulfilled by Jesus' death for the sins of the world. Jesus is here represented as the Passover lamb *par excellence*. In this light, the sacrifices of the Levitical system derive their meaning from their prefiguration of His death.

Then He blesses the bread, breaking and distributing it to His disciples, and saying, "Take, eat; this is My body which is given for you." He gives thanks for the wine and, offering the cup to His disciples, bids them, "Take this and divide it among yourselves" and "drink from it all of you . . . For this is My blood of the new covenant which is shed for many for the remission of sins . . . I will not drink of this fruit of the vine from now on until that day when I drink it new with you in My Father's kingdom." Having thus inaugurated the sacrament of the Eucharist on the night before His death, Jesus commands His disciples to enact it always "in remembrance of Me."

Upper Room Discourse

◀ John 14:1-31

Only John gives us an account of Jesus' final instruction to the disciples, often referred to as the Upper Room Discourse. Here Jesus deals with the disciples' fears about His impending death. He promises that He will prepare a place for them in His Father's house. The Holy Sprit will be with them until the day He returns.

He outlines the nature and ministry of the Holy Spirit: the Comforter Who will abide with the believer forever (14:16); the Spirit of truth Who will dwell *with* and *in* the believer (14:17); the Comforter Who will teach the believer and bring to remembrance all that Jesus has taught (14:26). Jesus tells His disciples these things in advance that they may have peace. Then Jesus and His disciples depart the Upper Room for the Garden of Gethsemane.

57 FROM THE UPPER ROOM TO GETHSEMANE

John 15:1–John 16:33 ▶

The Discourse Continued

On their way to the garden Jesus tells His disciples that He is "the true vine." Their fruitfulness depends on their faithfulness to abide in Him and continue to walk in His Spirit each day. Jesus reminds them that they are called and ordained by God, and that whatever they need to accomplish the tasks God gives them will be provided when they ask for them in His name. He warns that they will suffer rejection just as He has, but promises the comfort of the Holy Spirit.

Jesus tells His disciples that the Father will send them the Holy Spirit. He is the Spirit of truth, and He will testify of Jesus (15:26). Before the Spirit can be sent Jesus must first depart (16:7). The Spirit will convict the world of sin, righteousness, and judgment (16:8-11), and guide the disciples into all truth (16:13). He will reveal to the disciples the things to come (16:13), and will glorify Jesus by explaining His teachings to them (16:14).

The disciples are at a loss to understand the implications of what Jesus is saying, but Jesus promises they will soon understand everything. For now He speaks to them in proverbs. He has come from the Father into the world and must soon return. The world will rejoice while they will have great sorrow and though they will desert Him He will not be alone because the Father is with Him.

John 17:1-26 ▶

Jesus' High Priestly Prayer

Jesus asks His Father to glorify Him that He might in turn glorify His Father. The work He was given is now complete. He prays for the glory He had before the world began. Then Jesus prays for His disciples (17:6-26). In these 21 verses He makes reference to the disciples over 40 times, interceding for their ministry in the world and for the disciples who will be raised up after them. This prayer is well worth detailed study and consideration.

Matthew 26:30, 36-46 ▶
Mark 14:26, 32-42 ▶
Luke 22:39-46 ▶
John 18:1 ▶

Jesus' Prayer in the Garden of Gethsemane

Matthew and Mark indicate that the group sings a hymn on the way from the Upper Room to the Garden of Gethsemane on the Mount of Olives. The hymn would have come from Psalms 113–118, the group of psalms known as the Hallel and traditionally sung during the Passover celebration. Having crossed the Kidron brook, they enter the garden, where Jesus instructs the disciples to "sit here while I go and pray." He bids only Peter, James, and John accompany Him. "My soul is exceedingly sorrowful, even to death," Jesus tells them. "Stay here and watch with me." He then goes a little further, about "a stone's throw, [and] fell on His face." "O My Father," Jesus prays, "all things are possible for You. Take this cup away from Me."

Even in this harrowing hour Jesus submits Himself to the will of God. "Nevertheless, not My will, but Yours be done," He prays. Luke writes that at this moment an angel "appeared to Him from heaven, strengthening Him." "Being in agony," Jesus prays more strenuously still, so that "His sweat became like great drops of blood falling down to the ground." Rising, Jesus returns to find His disciples "sleeping from sorrow." "What!" He says to Peter, "are you sleeping? . . . Could you not watch with me one hour?"

"Rise and pray," He adjures His groggy followers, "lest you enter into temptation." When He returns from prayer to find them asleep again He rouses them once more. "Why do you sleep?" He chides them. The disciples' "eyes were heavy," and they "did not know what to answer Him." "Behold, the hour is at hand," He says, having returned from prayer and found them sleeping yet again, "the Son of Man is being betrayed into the hands of sinners.

Betrayal and Arrest

As Jesus gathers the disciples together, Judas arrives in the company of a great multitude bearing lanterns, torches, swords, and clubs. He has prearranged a sign to identify Jesus for His captors in the darkness of the garden: "Whomever I kiss, He is the One; seize Him."

"Greetings, Rabbi," Judas hails Jesus. "Friend," Jesus greets him, "why have you come?" Judas kisses Jesus. "Are you betraying the Son of Man with a kiss?" Jesus asks. John writes that, "knowing all things that would come upon Him," Jesus turns to the crowd. "Whom are You seeking?" He asks. "Jesus of Nazareth," they reply. "I am He," He answers. At this the crowd draws back and falls to the ground. "Whom are you seeking?" Jesus asks them again. "Jesus of Nazareth" the mob replies. "I have told you that I am He," Jesus says. "Therefore, if you seek Me let these others go their way."

At this Simon Peter draws his sword and strikes Malchus, the servant of the high priest, severing his right ear. "Put your sword into the sheath," Jesus rebukes Peter. "For all who take the sword will perish by the sword . . . Shall I not drink the cup which My Father has given Me? . . . Or do you think that I cannot now pray to My Father, and He will provide Me with more than twelve legions of angels?"

"Permit even this," Jesus says, touching Malchus' ear and restoring it. "Have you come out, as against a robber, with swords and clubs?" Jesus asks the crowd. "When I was with you daily in the temple, you did not try to seize Me. But this is your hour, and the power of darkness." Even so, all that is happening is done "that the Scriptures of the prophets might be fulfilled." Mark writes that at this moment Jesus' disciples "forsook Him and fled." He records the curious detail of "a certain young man" who followed Him. He is clad only in "a linen cloth" which he abandons when the crowd attempts to seize him, fleeing naked into the night.

Friday 1:00–3:00 A.M.
◄ Matthew 26:47-56
◄ Mark 14:43-52
◄ Luke 22:47-53
◄ John 18:2-12

107

4:00–6:00 A.M.

John 18:12-14, 19-23 ▶

58   FROM GETHSEMANE TO ANNAS' HOUSE

Examination Before Annas

Before dawn on Friday morning, Jesus is bound and arrested. He is conveyed first to the father-in-law of the High Priest Caiaphas, whose name is Annas. Annas questions Jesus about "His disciples and His doctrine."

"In secret I have said nothing," Jesus answers. "Why do you ask Me? Ask those who have heard Me." At this, one of the attending officers strikes Jesus "with the palm of his hand." "Do you answer the high priest like that?" he demands. "If I have spoken evil, bear witness of the evil," Jesus says to the officer, "but if well, why do you strike Me?"

59   FROM ANNAS TO CAIAPHAS THE HIGH PRIEST AND THE SANHEDRIN

Matthew 26:57, 59-68 ▶
Mark 14:53, 55-65 ▶
Luke 22:54, 63-65 ▶
John 18:24 ▶

Examination before Caiaphas

Jesus faces examination a second time before the High Priest Caiaphas and the assembled Sanhedrin. At this hearing a number of witnesses are produced to testify against Him. "This fellow said, 'I am able to destroy the temple of God,'" one witness charges. "We heard Him say 'I will build another made without hands.'" Mark writes that though several false witnesses malign Him their charges are inconsistent and contradictory.

Failing to establish a unified case with unassailable charges, the High Priest remains undeterred. "Do you answer nothing?" Caiaphas berates Him. "What is it these men testify against You?" Jesus holds His tongue, refusing to be provoked. "I put You under oath by the living God," Caiaphas terrorizes Jesus. "Are You the Christ, the Son of the Blessed?" "I am," replies Jesus. "And you will see the Son of Man sitting at the right hand of Power, and coming with the clouds of heaven." At this, Caiaphas tears his clothes crying, "What further need do we have of witnesses? . . . You have heard the blasphemy! What do you think?"

"He is deserving of death," the others answer. A brutal scene follows in which "they spat in His face and beat Him." He is blindfolded and the officers smite Him, jeering: "Prophesy to us, Christ! Who is the one who struck You?"

Denial by Peter

Matthew 26:58, 69-75 ▶
Mark 14:54, 66-72 ▶
Luke 22:54-62 ▶
John 18:15-18, 25-27 ▶

Meanwhile Peter, who has followed the crowd into a courtyard outside the trial room, warms himself with a few others around a fire. There a servant girl of the high priest recognizes him. "You also were with Jesus of Galilee," she says to him. Peter's denial is vehement: "I neither know nor understand what you are saying." "This is one of them," the servant girl assures the others standing around the fire. "I do not know the man," Peter insists. "Surely you are one of them," they say to Peter, "for you are a Galilean, and your speech shows it." At this Peter begins to "curse and swear." "I do not know this man of whom you speak," he rails at them. These words are scarcely spoken when Peter hears the sound of the rooster crowing and remembers Jesus' prediction that "before the rooster crows, you will deny Me three times." At this moment Jesus turns and looks at him and Peter flees the courtyard, weeping bitterly.

Final Condemnation by the Sanhedrin

At daylight the Sanhedrin reconvenes in an effort to legalize their proceedings. They ask Jesus whether He is the Christ. "If I tell you, you will by no means believe," Jesus replies. He tells them that they will see the Son of Man "seated at the right hand of God." The judges ask Him if He is claiming to be the Son of God. "It is as you have said," Jesus answers. With this confession, the religious leaders of Israel formally condemn Him.

6:00–6:30 A.M.
◀ Matthew 27:1
◀ Mark 15:1
◀ Luke 22:66-71

Death of Judas

In Matthew's account we find Judas, guilt-ridden, returning to the Temple and finding that Jesus has been condemned. "I have sinned by betraying innocent blood," Judas cries, throwing down before the chief priests and elders the 30 pieces of blood money. "What is that to us?" is their chilling reply, "You see to it." Judas flees the Temple and hangs himself. Luke adds the gruesome detail that "falling headlong, he burst open in the middle and all his entrails gushed out" (Acts 1:18-19). The priests use the money to buy a field in which to bury strangers. It is fittingly called *Akel Dama*, or *Field of Blood*. This development is itself prefigured by the prophet Jeremiah who writes, "And they took the thirty pieces of silver, the value of Him who was priced, whom they of the children of Israel priced, and gave them for the potter's field" (see Jeremiah 32:6-9).

◀ Matthew 27:3-10
◀ Acts 1:18-19

60 CAIAPHAS' PALACE TO PILATE'S HALL

Trial before Pilate

Because the Jewish leaders cannot legally put Jesus to death, they deliver Him bound from Caiaphas to the Roman Praetorium early that morning. "What accusation do you bring against this Man?" the Roman governor Pilate asks them. "If He were not an evildoer, we would not have delivered Him up to you," they reply. "You take Him and judge Him according to your law," Pilate tells them. "We found this fellow perverting the nation, and forbidding to pay taxes to Caesar, saying that He Himself is Christ, a King." Besides, they reason, "it is

6:30–7:00 A.M.
◀ Matthew 27:2, 11-14
◀ Mark 15:1-5
◀ Luke 23:1-5
◀ John 18:28-38

not lawful for us to put anyone to death." Reentering the Praetorium, Pilate summons Jesus. "Are you the king of the Jews?" Pilate asks Him. "Are you speaking for yourself," Jesus replies, "or did others tell you this?" "Am I a Jew?" Pilate fires back. "Your own nation and the chief priests have delivered You to me. What have you done?" "My kingdom is not of this world," Jesus says. "Are you a king, then?" Pilate demands. "It is as you say," Jesus replies. "For this cause I was born, and for this cause I have come into the world, that I should bear witness to the truth." "What is truth?" Pilate scoffs.

The Roman governor returns to the chief priests and the crowd. "I find no fault in Him at all," he tells them. "He stirs up the people, teaching throughout all Judea, beginning from Galilee to this place," the crowd insists. Pilate sees a way out of this dilemma when he learns that Jesus is from Galilee and dispatches Him under guard to King Herod, who owns the legal responsibility for the region.

7:00–7:30 A.M.

61 FROM PILATE TO HEROD

Luke 23:6-12 ▸

Trial before Herod

Herod is delighted to have Jesus now under his jurisdiction since "he desired for a long time to see Him." Hoping to see some kind of miracle from Him, "he questioned Him with many words." Jesus answers him nothing. Eventually, Herod with his "men of war" begins to mock Jesus, treating Him with contempt. Before returning Him to Pilate they have Him "arrayed in a gorgeous robe." Luke records that although Herod and Pilate had been "at enmity with each other," they are reconciled on this day.

7:30–8:00 A.M.

62 FROM HEROD BACK TO PILATE

Matthew 27:15-26 ▸
Mark 15:6-15 ▸
Luke 23:13-25 ▸
John 18:39-40 ▸
John 19:1, 4-16 ▸

Second Trial before Pilate

"You have brought this Man to me, as one who misleads the people," says Pilate to the crowd, having received Jesus back under his custody. "And indeed, having examined Him in your presence, I have found no fault in this Man concerning those things of which you accuse him."

"No, neither did Herod," Pilate continues, "for I sent you back to him, and indeed nothing deserving of death has been done by Him. I will therefore chastise Him and then release Him." "Away with this man," the crowd cries. "Crucify Him!"

Mark writes that at this time "there was one named Barabbas who was chained with his fellow rebels" because "they had committed murder in the rebellion." "You have a custom," Pilate says to the crowd, "that I should release someone to you at the Passover." Pilate is beginning to think that the best way to resolve the stalemate is to let the crowd decide between Jesus and Barrabas. One of them may be released in accordance with a custom setting free a condemned man each year at Passover. "Do you want me therefore to release to you the King of the Jews?" He says.

At this moment a message arrives from Pilate's wife. "Have nothing to do with this just man," she urges her husband, "for I have suffered many things today in a dream because of Him." Even failing to comprehend the awful historical moment of this scene, Pilate finds himself in something of a predicament. "Sitting in the seat of judgment," a place called *The Pavement* or in Hebrew *Gabbatha*, He is confronted at once with two horns of a dilemma. Pilate knows "that they had handed Him over because of envy" and that Jesus should therefore be acquitted but "he saw that he could not prevail" over the murderous demands of the crowd and "that a tumult was rising." "Which of these two do you want me to release to You?" Pilate offers, indicating Jesus and Barabbas. "Not this man, but Barabbas!" the crowd answers. "What shall I do with Jesus who is called the Christ?" He demands. "Let Him be crucified," they cry.

Pilate has Jesus taken out and scourged. "I am bringing Him out to you," Pilate says to the crowd, "that you may know that I find no fault in Him."

"Behold the Man," he says to mob, as Jesus emerges, wearing the crown of thorns and clad in a scarlet robe. "Crucify Him! Crucify Him!" the chief priests and officers cry. "You take Him and crucify Him!" Pilate snaps. "For I find no fault in Him." "We have a law," the Jews answer, "and according to our law He ought to die, because He made Himself the Son of God."

At this, Pilate takes fright and reenters the Praetorium with Jesus. "Where are you from?" Pilate asks Him. Jesus remains silent. "Are you not speaking to me?" Pilate demands, incredulous. "Do you not know that I have power to crucify You, and power to release You?" "You could have no power at all against Me unless it had been given you from above," Jesus answers. John writes that at this Pilate makes another attempt to release Jesus but is overcome by the murderous crowd. "If you let this Man go, you are not Caesar's friend," they tell him. "Whoever makes himself a king speaks against Caesar."

"Behold your king!" Pilate says to them, baiting them from his judgment seat. "Away with Him, away with Him! Crucify Him!" the crowd cries. "Shall I crucify Your King?" Pilate demands. "We have no king but Caesar," the chief priests answer.

Pilate calls for water to wash his hands as a sign absolving himself. "I am innocent of the blood of this just person," he tells them. At this "all the people answered and said, 'His blood be on us and on our children.'"

Roman Mockery

Matthew 27:27-30 ▶
Mark 15:16-19 ▶
John 19:2-3 ▶

The Roman soldiers lead Jesus to the Praetorium court where He suffers further abuse. In His right hand they place a reed. "Hail, King of the Jews!" they taunt Him as they "struck Him on the head" and "spat on Him." Matthew writes that "bowing the knee they worshiped Him," a mocking and blasphemous tribute.

8:00–9:00 A.M.

63 FROM PILATE'S HALL TO GOLGOTHA

The Via Dolorosa

Matthew 27:31-34 ▶
Mark 15:20-23 ▶
Luke 23:26-33 ▶
John 19:16-17 ▶

The soldiers strip Jesus for crucifixion and lead Him to Golgotha. This path is known as the *Via Dolorosa*, or *way of sorrow*. Jesus is so weakened by the beatings and flogging that He is unable to carry His cross. The soldiers conscript "Simon the Cyrenian, [a man] coming out of the country and passing by" to carry the cross to the *Place of the Skull*, or *Golgotha*. A crowd follows "and women who also mourned and lamented Him."

"Daughters of Jerusalem," Jesus says to them, "do not weep for Me, but weep for yourselves and for your children. For indeed the days are coming in which they will say, 'Blessed are the barren wombs that never bore, and breasts which never nursed!' [and] to the mountains, 'Fall on us!' and to the hills, 'Cover us! . . . For if they do these things in the green wood, what will be done in the dry?" Two thieves are crucified with Jesus. A wine mixed with anaesthetic is offered Him but He refuses it.

The Crucifixion

9:00 A.M.–12:00 P.M.
Matthew 27:35-44 ▶
Mark 15:24-32 ▶
Luke 23:33-43 ▶
John 19:18-27 ▶

Following Mark's account, the soldiers nail Jesus to the cross and hang Him up to die between the two thieves. ***Father, forgive them, for they do not know what they do***," Jesus prays. After dividing His clothes among them, the soldiers at the foot of the cross negotiate for His tunic "which was without seam, woven from the top in one piece."

"Let us not tear it but cast lots for it, whose it shall be," the soldiers agree. This is an unwitting fulfillment of King David's prophecy that "they divide my garments among them, and for My clothing they cast lots" (see Psalm 22:18). Pilate orders an inscription hung over Jesus written in "letters of Greek, Latin and Hebrew."

"This is Jesus, the King of the Jews," the sign proclaims. The chief priests object to the sign: "Do not write, 'The King of the Jews,' but 'He said, I am the King of the Jews.'" Pilate baldly refuses to amend it. "What I have written, I have written," he says, dismissing them.

The religious leaders and the people passing by rail at Jesus, "wagging their heads" and blaspheming Him. "Let the Christ, the King of

Israel, descend now from the cross, that we may see and believe," they taunt. "You who would destroy the temple and build it in three days, save Yourself! If You are the Son of God, come down from the cross." The chief priests, scribes, and elders join the chorus of abuse: "He saved others; let Him save Himself if He is the Christ, the chosen of God."

Even one of the thieves with whom He is crucified taunts Him: "If You are the Christ, save yourself and us." The other rebukes him. "Do you not even fear God, seeing that you are under the same condemnation? We receive the due reward of our deeds; but this Man has done nothing wrong." Turning to Jesus he says, "Lord, remember me when You come into Your kingdom." *"Assuredly, I say to you,"* Jesus replies, *"today you will be with Me in Paradise."*

Gathered at the foot of the cross are Jesus' mother "and her sister, Mary the wife of Clopas," together with Mary Magdalene and the disciple John. Jesus commends His mother to John's care. *"Woman, behold your son!"* He says to her. *"Behold your mother!"* He says to John. The Gospel writer records that "from that hour the disciple took her to his own home."

The Great Darkness

Jesus has been on the cross for three hours when a great darkness covers the land. The darkness lasts from the sixth to the ninth hour. Then Jesus cries: *"'Eloi, Eloi, lama sabachthani?'* which is translated *'My God, My God, why have you forsaken Me?'"* (Psalm 22:1). The words are taken from a psalm of King David. "This Man is calling for Elijah!" some of those standing near the cross erroneously observe.

"I thirst," Jesus says. One of the bystanders runs to fetch a sponge and soaking it in sour wine raises it to Jesus' lips on the end of a hyssop reed. "Let Him alone," the others say, "let us see if Elijah will come to take Him down." *"It is finished,"* Jesus says in a loud voice. His passion on the cross is complete. His last breath is spent in a prayer: *"Father, into your hands I commit My spirit."*

The Death of Jesus

At the moment of Jesus' death, the curtain in the Temple that veiled the Holy of Holies is rent in two from top to bottom, signifying the direct access to God through Christ (see Hebrews 4:14-16). Matthew records that "the earth quaked, and the rocks were split and the graves were opened." From the tombs proceed "the bodies of the saints" raised from the dead. These saints go into the Holy City where they appear after His resurrection to many. Upon witnessing these events, a centurion and those with him are filled with fear. "Truly this was the Son of God!" the centurian confesses.

12:00–3:00 P.M.
◄ Matthew 27:45-50
◄ Mark 15:33-37
◄ Luke 23:44-46
◄ John 19:28-30

3:00 P.M.
◄ Matthew 27:51-56
◄ Mark 15:38-41
◄ Luke 23:45, 47-49

64 FROM GOLGOTHA TO JOSEPH'S TOMB

3:00–6:00 P.M.

Matthew 27:57-60 ▶
Mark 15:42-46 ▶
Luke 23:50-54 ▶
John 19:31-42 ▶

Jesus' Burial

According to Mosaic Law, it is unlawful to leave a dead person unburied on the Sabbath (see Deuteronomy 21:22-23, Exodus 34:24). The religious leaders ask Pilate that the legs of the three crucified men be broken to hasten death and allow for burial to take place before sunset. Pilate consents and the soldiers enact the brutal chore, breaking the legs of the thieves crucified alongside Jesus first. When the soldiers come to Jesus they find that He is already dead. It is thus unnecessary to break His legs. This is in accordance with a prophecy in the Psalms: "He guards all His bones, not even one of them is broken" (see Psalm 34:20). One of the soldiers pierces Jesus' side with his spear, in fulfillment of the prophet Zechariah who wrote, "Then they will look on Me whom they pierced" (Zechariah 12:10). From the wound flow "blood and water."

Joseph of Arimathea, a Jewish religious leader and disciple of Jesus, asks Pilate for permission to bury Jesus' body. Assured by his soldiers that Jesus is dead, Pilate releases His body to Joseph, who with help from Nicodemus prepares it for burial. For this purpose Nicodemus brings with him "about a hundred pounds" of an embalming preparation, "a mixture of myrrh and aloes." This is used when they bind the body of Jesus in "strips of linen with the spices." The tomb "in which no one had yet been laid" is "hewn out of the rock" in a garden close to the site of His crucifixion. There they place Jesus' body. Then they roll a stone in front of its entrance and depart.

Saturday
Matthew 27:62-66 ▶

Pilate Secures the Tomb

The chief priests and the Pharisees "gathered together to Pilate" the following day. "Sir," they say to him, "we remember, while He was still alive, how that deceiver said, 'After three days I will rise.' Therefore command that the tomb be made secure until the third day, lest His disciples come by night and steal Him away, and say to the people, 'He has risen from the dead.'" If this happens, "the last deception will be worst than the first." "You have a guard," Pilate answers, "go your way, make it as secure as you know how." Jesus is buried late on Friday afternoon, before the beginning of the Sabbath. He remains in the tomb during the Sabbath.

Matthew 27:61,28:1 ▶
Mark 15:47-16:1 ▶
Luke 23:55-56 ▶

Preparation for Embalming

His mother and the other women see where Jesus is buried and return home to prepare spices and ointment for use after the Sabbath. Late Saturday Mary Magdalene, Mary the mother of James, and Salome gather the spices for anointing the body and begin their way back to the tomb. They are probably staying in Bethany, a few miles from the burial site.

Conclusion

On the eve of His death Jesus explains that the Holy Spirit will be sent to indwell His disciples, empowering them to fulfill their role as ministers of the Gospel. The sign of bread and wine at the Passover meal is fulfilled in Jesus' broken body and spilled blood.

Resurrection and Post-resurrection Ministry (40 Days)

This chapter records Jesus' resurrection from the dead and return to heaven from the Mount of Olives.

Spring, A.D. 30

The Earthquake

Matthew records that early on Sunday morning, before the women arrive, a great earthquake shakes the cemetery. An angel of the Lord, whose "countenance was like lightning" descends from heaven, rolls back the stone and sits down on it. His clothing is "as white as snow" and those guarding the tomb "shook for fear of him and became like dead men."

Sunday
◀ Matthew 28:2-4

The Women Enter the Tomb

As Mary Magdalene and "the other Mary" make their way to the tomb, they wonder how they will be able to move the stone that seals its entrance. As they near the tomb they see that the stone has already been rolled away. There they are greeted by an angel. "I know that you seek Jesus who was crucified," the angel says. "He is not here; for He is risen, as He said." The Gospels record that Jesus has told His disciples on at least seven different occasions that He would rise from the dead.

◀ Matthew 28:5-8
◀ Mark 16:2-8
◀ Luke 24:1-8
◀ John 20:1

"Come, see the place where the Lord lay," the angel invites the women. "Go quickly and tell His disciples. He is risen from the dead, and indeed He is going before you into Galilee; there you will see Him." The astonished women flee in terror and joy to tell the others.

The Women Report to the Apostles

Mary arrives and begins to recount the angel's message to the disciples. At first, the disciples refuse to believe the women since "their words seemed to them like idle tales," but Peter then takes off running for the tomb, followed by John. John overtakes him and arrives at the tomb first. When Peter arrives he enters the tomb where he finds Jesus' linen burial shroud but no body. The veil that covered Jesus' head is folded and set to one side. John and Peter depart, pondering the implications of their discovery. The resurrection is still largely a mystery to them.

◀ Luke 24:9-12
◀ John 20:2-10

65 RESURRECTION TO THE ASCENSION

Jesus Appears to Mary

Meanwhile, Mary Magdalene returns to the tomb, where she meets two angels. "Woman, why are you weeping," they ask her. "Because they have taken away my Lord, and I do not know where they have laid Him," Mary answers. At this moment she turns and sees Jesus. "Whom are you seeking?" Jesus asks. Mistaking Him for the gardener Mary answers: "Sir, if you have carried Him away, tell me where you have laid Him, and I will take Him away." "Mary," Jesus says to her. "Rabboni!" she says, recognizing Him at last. "Do not cling to Me," Jesus tells her, "for I have not yet ascended to My Father; but go to My brethren and say to them, 'I am ascending to My Father and your Father, and to My God and your God.'" Mary returns to the disciples and tells them about Jesus' appearance and "that He had spoken these things to her."

Jesus Appears to the Other Women

Some of the other women returning to the tomb encounter Jesus on the road. "Rejoice," Jesus tells them. At this they "held Him by the feet and worshiped Him." Jesus instructs them to pass the word to the disciples that He will meet with them in Galilee.

Confusion among the Guards

While these events transpire, the soldiers assigned to guard the tomb report to the chief priest. The elders are called to confer about what should be done. Offering a large sum of money, they instruct the soldiers to report that "His disciples came at night and stole Him away while we slept." Since Pilate would no doubt punish these soldiers for sleeping on the job, the elders promise to intervene on their behalf. "If this comes to the governor's ears, we will appease him and make you secure," they promise. The guards take the money and do as they are told.

The Appearance on the Road to Emmaus

Late on Sunday afternoon Jesus joins two disciples walking on the road to Emmaus. The two are discussing Jesus' death and the reports of His resurrection. "What kind of conversation is this that you have with one another as you walk and are sad?" Jesus inquires. "Are you the only stranger in Jerusalem, and have You not known the things which have happened there in these days?" Cleopas answers, clearly failing to recognize Him. "What things?" Jesus asks. "The things concerning Jesus of Nazareth, who was a prophet mighty in deed and word before God and all the people," they reply.

The two rehearse for Jesus the events of the last week. "But we were hoping that it was He who was going to restore Israel." They tell Him of certain unsubstantiated reports of a missing body and "a vision of angels who said He was alive."

"O foolish ones," Jesus says to them, "and slow of heart to believe in all that the prophets have spoken! Ought not the Christ to have suffered these things and to enter into His glory?" He then begins to expound for them, "beginning at Moses and all the Prophets . . . the things concerning Himself."

When the three reach Emmaus, the two disciples invite Him to stay the night with them: "Abide with us, for it is toward evening, and the day is far spent." At dinner that evening Jesus breaks the bread and blesses it and at this moment the disciples recognize that it is He. Suddenly, Jesus vanishes from their sight. "Did not our heart burn within us while He talked with us on the road, and while He opened the Scriptures to us?" they exclaim.

Report from Emmaus

The two disciples get up and return to Jerusalem to report to the others, whom they find discussing Peter's personal encounter with Jesus earlier in the day. We have no record of this encounter apart from the reference in Luke and Paul's reference to it in 1 Corinthians 15:5. The two disciples who have arrived from Emmaus recount their meeting with Jesus.

Sunday Afternoon
4th Resurrection Appearance
◄ Luke 24:33-35

Appearance to the Disciples

As the two are giving their account, Jesus suddenly appears in the midst of them even though the doors and windows remain closed and locked for fear of the religious authorities. "Peace be unto you," Jesus says. He chides them for their unwillingness to believe the reports of His resurrection. "Why are you troubled? And why do doubts arise in your hearts?" Jesus asks. "Behold My hands and My feet, that it is I Myself. Handle Me and see, for a spirit does not have flesh and bones as you see I have." The disciples can scarcely believe what is happening. "Have you any food here?" Jesus asks. The disciples give him "a piece of broiled fish and some honeycomb" which Jesus eats in their presence.

Sunday Afternoon
5th Resurrection Appearance
◄ Mark 16:14
◄ Luke 24:36-43
◄ John 20:19-25

"As the Father sent Me," Jesus charges them, "I also send you." He gives them a special anointing of His Spirit until the coming of the Holy Spirit at the Feast of Pentecost (Shavuot). Thomas is absent during this appearance and refuses to accept the testimony of the other disciples. "Unless I see in His hands the print of nails," he tells them, "and put my finger into the print of nails, and put my hand into His side, I will not believe."

Jesus' Encounter with Thomas

One week later, with Thomas present, Jesus appears to His disciples again. "Reach your finger here," Jesus says to Thomas, "and look at My hands; and reach your hand here, and put it into My side. Do not

Sunday, One week later
6th Resurrection Appearance
◄ John 20:26-31

119

be unbelieving, but believe." "My Lord and my God!" Thomas answers. "Thomas, because you have seen Me, you have believed," Jesus says. "Blessed are those who have not seen and yet have believed." John notes that Jesus did many other signs that the Gospel writers did not record.

Appearance to the Seven beside the Sea of Galilee

7th Resurrection Appearance
John 21:1-25 ▶

The disciples depart Jerusalem and return to their homes in Galilee. "I am going fishing," Peter tells the others. James, John, Thomas, Nathanael, and two others decide to join him. The disciples fish the night away, but catch nothing. "Children," Jesus calls to them from the shore the following morning, "have you any food?" "No," the disciples answer, not recognizing Him. "Cast the net on the right side of the boat," Jesus tells them, "and you will find some." The disciples do as they are told and instantly a school of fish enters the nets so large they are "not able to draw it in."

"It is the Lord," John exclaims to Peter. Peter hastily puts on "his outer garment (for he had removed it), and plunged into the sea." The rest of the disciples put to shore in the little boat "dragging the net with fish." When they land they find Jesus with a "fire of coals there, and fish laid on it and bread."

"Bring some of the fish which you have caught," Jesus says. Peter drags the unbroken net full of large fish to land. "Come and eat breakfast," Jesus invites His disciples. After breakfast, Jesus says to Peter, "Simon, son of Jonah, do you love Me more than these?" "Yes, Lord," Peter answers, "you know that I love You." "Feed My lambs," Jesus tells him. "Simon, son of Jonah," Jesus says to him again, "do you love Me?" "Yes, Lord," Peter replies, "You know that I love You." "Tend My sheep," Jesus says. When Jesus asks Peter a third time, "Simon, son of Jonah, do you love Me?" Peter is cut to the heart. "Lord, you know all things," Peter says, "You know that I love You." "Feed My sheep," Jesus replies.

"Most assuredly, I say to you," Jesus says to Peter, "when you were younger, you girded yourself and walked where you wished; but when you are old, you will stretch out your hands, and another will gird you and carry you where you do not wish." By these words to Peter Jesus foretells "by what death he would glorify God."

"But, Lord," Peter says to Him, indicating the disciple John, "what about this man?" "If I will that he remain till I come, what is that to you?" Jesus answers. "You follow Me."

John closes his Gospel with the observation that Jesus did and said many other things that are not recorded and that "the world itself could not contain the books that would be written" if they were.

8th Resurrection Appearance
◀ Matthew 28:16-20

The Great Commission

Several of the post-resurrection events fit together only awkwardly. The Broadus and Robertson harmonies place Mark 16:15-18 and I Corinthians 15:6 with Matthew 28:16-20, but we have listed these events in separate accounts.

Matthew tells us that the eleven disciples are appointed to meet Jesus on a mountain near the Sea of Galilee, where Jesus gives them the Great Commission. Here Jesus promises to be their resource. Whatever they need to accomplish their task, He has both the power and authority to give. The imperative of the Great Commission is to "make disciples of all the nations, baptizing them in the name of the Father, and of the Son, and of the Holy Spirit." Jesus promises to be with the disciples "to the end of the age."

◀ I Corinthians 15:6

Appearance to the 500

Some scholars believe Jesus' appearance to the eleven and to the 500 witnesses mentioned in 1 Corinthians refer to the same event. Matthew tells us only about the eleven present when Jesus gives the Great Commission. Paul tells us about an appearance to 500 witnesses without giving us specifics.

Appearance to James

9th Resurrection Appearance
◀ Mark 16:15-18
◀ I Corinthians 15:7

The 40 days of Jesus' post-resurrection appearances are almost over. Jesus meets with His disciples again, commanding them to "go into all the world and preach the gospel." He promises them the continuing testimony of miraculous signs. Paul relates that Jesus also appeared to His half-brother James, who will become one of the leaders of the early church in Jerusalem (1 Corinthians 15:7).

Final Appearance and Instruction

10th Resurrection Appearance
◀ Luke 24:44-49
◀ Acts 1:3-8

At the end of the 40 days, Jesus meets with the disciples for the last time before His ascension. He reviews the Old Testament prophecies and explains to the disciples how these have been fulfilled in His life, death, and resurrection. With this knowledge the disciples will be able to teach other disciples they will themselves raise up. Jesus reminds them to "tarry in Jerusalem until you are endued with power from on high." Their mission is to preach the Gospel in Jerusalem and carry its message to all the nations of the earth.

The Ascension

◀ Mark 16:19-20
◀ Luke 24:50-53
◀ Acts 1:9-12

Jesus then leads His disciples onto the Mount of Olives, where He begins to ascend until a cloud receives Him out of their sight. Stunned, the disciples stand looking up into the sky until two men appear in white apparel. "Men of Galilee," they greet them, "why do you stand gazing up into heaven? This same Jesus, who was taken up from you into heaven, will so come in like manner as you saw Him go into heaven." They return to Jerusalem and ten days later, at the feast of Pentecost (Shavuot), the promised Spirit of God clothes the disciples with power just as John the Baptist foretold in the days before Jesus began His public ministry (see Luke 3:16).

The power of the Holy Spirit transforms the eleven fearful disciples into eleven men who in the face of death take the Gospel to the nations of the world.

Conclusion

During the 40 days between His resurrection and ascension Jesus explains to His disciples all that has just transpired — things He had warned them of beforehand but which they were unable to comprehend. His final accomplishment comes at Pentecost, when He baptizes His followers with the fire of the Spirit of God, who comes to indwell the disciples and empower them to fulfill the Great Commission.

AUTHOR'S POSTSCRIPT

Y ou have just completed a study of the life and ministry of Jesus Christ. We have examined the events surrounding His birth, His childhood and His years of public ministry - ending with His death, resurrection and ascension back into Heaven.

In writing this book my co-authors and I have endeavored to simply trace the amazing events of Christ's life in chronological order, harmonizing the four Gospel accounts into one linear narrative. Although theological and philosophical opinions vary on many of these events, we have tried to refrain from any personal "spin" or bias, and to let the events speak for themselves as to their import and significance for us as individuals. As a postscript to this work, however, I do want to share a little of my own experience with the person of Jesus Christ.

As a child I attended church regularly and heard about Jesus every week, but these old and familiar stories had little relevance for me. As a teenager I turned my back on the church and lived a life that was contrary to everything I had been taught as a child. At age twenty, however, I realized that my strategy for living my life "on my own" apart from God had only led me into alcoholism and two visits to jail.

Humbled and desperate, I cried out to God for help. Shortly thereafter I met a wonderful man who was able to explain to me who Jesus was, why He came to earth and why He died. He explained that Christ's life, death, and resurrection had been for the express purpose of restoring mankind - not to a religion, but to a relationship with God. He encouraged me to begin reading the Gospels so that I could discover for myself the amazing life of Christ.

On April 8, 1956, I made a life-changing personal decision - asking God to forgive my wrongs, to come into my heart and life and to help me become the person He had created me to be. As I continued to read the Bible daily, I discovered that I was actually experiencing a dialogue with God. He was speaking to me through His Word and I was speaking to Him in prayer. Gradually, I began to realize that I was developing that relationship with God that my friend had explained to me. Now, over four decades later, I can truly say that this relationship with God through Christ has become deeper and more precious with each passing day and has formed the foundation for my entire life.

It is my prayer that every reader of this book will encounter the person of Christ - not only as a historical figure - but also as a life-changing reality. If, after your reading and study of Christ's life through this book, you would like to explore further a relationship with God through Christ, I would be delighted to send you -- free of charge -- a book that focuses on the Gospel of John. It will guide you in your first 31 days of establishing a new relationship with God. If this would be of help to you, please feel free to contact our office and request the John Study. For a comprehensive picture of how Jesus' life and ministry is a consummation of the larger narrative of the scriptures see a *Visual Survey of the Bible,* the first book in this series, also available through ETS Ministries.

Every Blessing,

David L. Dawson

Ephesians 4:12 Ministries, Inc.
4400 Moulton St. Suite D
Greenville, TX 75401
Phone: 1-888-577-7739
Fax: 903 454-8524
Email: etsusa@aol.com

BIBLIOGRAPHY

Holy Bible, New King James Version, 1982.

John A. Broadus, *A Harmony of the Gospels in the Revised Version, with New Helps for Historical Study* (New York: A. C. Armstrong & Son, 1903).

J. Dwight Pentecost, *The Words and Works of Jesus Christ: A Study of the Life of Christ* (Grand Rapids, MI: Zondervan, 1981).

A. T. Robertson, *A Harmony of the Gospels* (New York: Harper & Brothers Publishers, 1922).

Dr. H. L. Willmington, *Willmington's Guide to the Bible* (Fort Washinton, PA: Christian Literature Crusade, 1995).

OTHER WORKS BY DAVID L. DAWSON

A Visual Survey of the Bible (available in Adult, Youth, and Children's editions)

Studies in John

Equipping the Saints Discipleship Training Guide, Volumes 1-4.
Volume 1-A *Establishing the Vision*
Volume 1-B *Building the Basics*
Volume 2-A *Evangelizing as a Lifestyle*
Volume 2-B *Conserving Evangelism's Fruit*
Volume 3-A *Discipling in Small Groups*
Volume 3-B *Reproducing Laborers*
Volume 4-A *Developing Leadership*
Volume 4-B *Mastering the Bible*

These works can be ordered from:
Equipping the Saints Ministries
4400 Moulton St. Suite D
Greenville, TX 75401
Ph. 1-888-577-7739
e-mail: etsusa@aol.com
www.equippingthesaints.org

Index

Chapter 7
The Training Of The Twelve and Others 61

Matthew 1:21

And she will bring forth a Son, and you shall call His name Jesus, for He will save His people from their sins.

NKJ

John 3:16

For God so loved the world that He gave His only begotten Son, that whoever believes in Him should not perish but have everlasting life.

NKJ

Matthew 4:19

Then He said to them, "Follow Me, and I will make you fishers of men."

NKJ

Matthew 6:33

But seek first the kingdom of God and His righteousness, and all these things shall be added to you.

NKJ

Matthew 9:37-38

Then He said to His disciples, "The harvest truly is plentiful, but the laborers are few. Therefore pray the Lord of the harvest to send out laborers into His harvest."

NKJ

Luke 9:23

Then He said to them all, "If anyone desires to come after Me, let him deny himself, and take up his cross daily, and follow Me."

NKJ

Mark 9:23

Jesus said to him, "If you can believe, all things are possible to him who believes."

NKJ

John 10:27-29

My sheep hear My voice, and I know them, and they follow Me. And I give them eternal life, and they shall never perish; neither shall anyone snatch them out of My hand. My Father, who has given them to Me, is greater than all; and no one is able to snatch them out of My Father's hand.

NKJ

Mark 10:45

For even the Son of Man did not come to be served, but to serve, and to give His life a ransom for many.

NKJ

John 13:34

A new commandment I give to you, that you love one another; as I have loved you, that you also love one another.

NKJ

John 1:12

But as many as received Him, to them He gave the right to become children of God, to those who believe in His name.

NKJ

Matthew 22:37-40

Jesus said to him, "'You shall love the Lord your God with all your heart, with all your soul, and with all your mind.' This is the first and great commandment. And the second is like it: 'You shall love your neighbor as yourself.' On these two commandments hang all the Law and the Prophets."

NKJ

Matthew 28:18-20

And Jesus came and spoke to them, saying, "All authority has been given to Me in heaven and on earth. Go therefore and make disciples of all the nations, baptizing them in the name of the Father and of the Son and of the Holy Spirit, teaching them to observe all things that I have commanded you; and lo, I am with you always, even to the end of the age."

NKJ